DOMAIN o6

MW00630241

MANAGEMENT

SMPS
PUBLICATIONS

www.smps.org

SMPS PUBLICATIONS is an imprint of the Society for Marketing Professional Services
123 N. Pitt Street, Suite 400, Alexandria, VA 22314

703.549.6117 | www.smps.org

SMPS is a not-for-profit, professional organization established to promote research and education that advances the body of knowledge in the field of professional services marketing and develops a greater understanding of the role and value of marketing in the A/E/C industry.

© 2016 by the Society for Marketing Professional Services (SMPS)®

SMPS is a registered service mark of the Society for Marketing Professional Services.

Cover Photo: Sound Transit Light Rail's UW Stadium Station construction, Seattle, WA; for Hoffman Construction.

© Andrew Buchanan, Subtle Light Photography / subtlelightphoto.com

Book design and layout: MilesHerndon / milesherndon.com

Domain 6: Management

MARKENDIUM: SMPS Body of Knowledge

Library of Congress Control Number: 2016945980

ISBN-13: 978-0-9974818-3-9 (Paperback)

ISBN-13: 978-0-9974818-4-6 (EPUB)

10 9 8 7 6 5 4 3 2 1

Published in the United States of America

First Edition | First Printing

SMPS PUBLICATIONS are available for sale on most online retailers in the U.S., U.K., Canada and Australia. Books are also available to the trade through Ingram and Amazon.com. For more information, contact info@smps.org.

THE SOCIETY FOR MARKETING PROFESSIONAL SERVICES (SMPS) is a community of marketing and business development professionals working to secure profitable business relationships for their A/E/C companies. Through networking, business intelligence, and research, SMPS members gain a competitive advantage in positioning their firms successfully in the marketplace. SMPS offers members professional development, leadership opportunities, and marketing resources to advance their careers.

SMPS is the only organization dedicated to creating business opportunities in the A/E/C industry. Companies tap into a powerful national and regional network to form teams, secure business referrals and intelligence, and benchmark performance. SMPS was created in 1973 by a small group of professional services firm leaders who recognized the need to sharpen skills, pool resources, and work together to build their businesses.

Today, SMPS represents a dynamic network of almost 7,000 marketing and business development professionals from architectural, engineering, planning, interior design, construction, and specialty consulting firms located throughout the United States and Canada. The Society and its chapters benefit from the support of 3,700 design and building firms, encompassing 80 percent of the Engineering News-Record Top 500 Design Firms and Top 400 Contractors.

For more information, visit our website at:
www.smps.org

PUT THE DOMAINS TO WORK FOR YOU AND YOUR FIRM.

This comprehensive, six-book series further defines the six Domains of Practice for SMPS and the A/E/C industries. Learn more at smps.org/markendium—and take your firm's marketing and business development efforts to the next level.

Now available for purchase on Amazon.

For more info:
smps.org/markendium

MARKENDIUM
SMPS BODY OF KNOWLEDGE

The MARKENDIUM: SMPS Body of Knowledge (BOK) is the premier go-to learning resource for the successful practice of marketing and business development in the A/E/C professions. The MARKENDIUM: BOK is not a singular publication or a catalog of ideas. It is inclusive of the contemporary knowledge necessary for thriving careers and firms in these professions and beyond.

The MARKENDIUM: BOK was curated in a collaborative way by experts in the A/E/C professions and is a compilation of existing and newly sourced content. The MARKENDIUM: BOK is built on the foundation of the six Domains of Practice identified by SMPS:

Marketing Research

Marketing Planning

Client and Business Development

Proposals

Promotional Activity

Management

Icon Legend

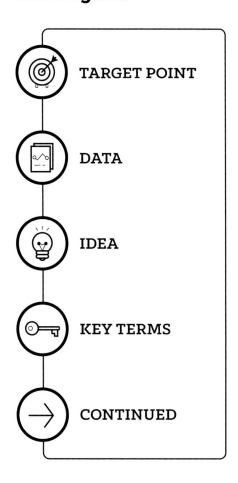

TARGET POINT

DATA

IDEA

KEY TERMS

CONTINUED

Domain 6: Management

Navigation Menu

MANAGEMENT

Introduction

MARKENDIUM: The SMPS body of knowledge for Professional Services Marketers is classified under six Domains of Practice. These Domains of Practice are as follows:

Domain 1: Marketing Research

Marketing research is executed to gather, record, and analyze data related to marketing a firm's services. The data can be used to identify and define marketing opportunities; generate, refine, and evaluate marketing actions; monitor marketing performance; and forecast trends.

Domain 2: Marketing Planning

The marketing plan serves as a map to define a firm's market prospects and key market characteristics. The plan should include marketing goals and strategies to ensure successful direction to the team, as well as information on how marketing budgets and efforts should be spent.

Domain 3: Client and Business Development

Business development involves relationship building with current and prospective clients, often prior to a request for proposal. Through interaction with the client, development activities may include calls, visits, correspondence, social media, referrals, and tradeshows.

Domain 4: Proposals

Proposals are prepared in response to a specific solicitation where the project and scope of work are identified. Proposals can include general firm information, relevant projects, a technical project approach, and key staff résumés.

Domain 5: Promotional Activity

This undertaking includes all forms of communications and inbound/outbound marketing. Some examples include advertising, direct mail, website, social media, brochures, presentations, special events, public relations, and news releases.

Domain 6: Management

Management involves coordinating the efforts of staff and/or consultants to accomplish marketing goals and objectives. Using available resources, management effectively plans, organizes, staffs, and directs projects of an organization or firm.

As mentioned above, this sixth Domain, Management, covers coordinating the efforts of staff and consultants to accomplish marketing goals and objectives. This section discusses the basics of staff management, from setting clear expectations and providing training and mentoring opportunities to establishing clear lines of communication and providing regular feedback. It covers the importance of internal communications, and how to use the sales pipeline to update the company on wins, losses and proposal generation. This section also addresses the reliance of market effectiveness on knowledge management systems; in particular, the customer relationship management (CRM) system.

We'll discuss how you can train your marketing professionals to step up to a business development (BD) role, and how participation in professional organizations can be a path to personal development as well as a means to generate new business. We'll look at ways to attract talent to your organization, and the importance of presenting your company as an attractive place to work. This section also covers basic accounting and contracting principles, and discusses their relevance to your role in marketing. Finally, we'll talk about ways to promote a firm-wide BD culture, and the effect that can have on the firm's success.

1   Supervise Marketing and Support Staff

Managing people may be as much an art as it is a science, but there are many basic processes you can put into place to ensure the best possible outcomes for your staff's performance, from setting clear expectations and providing training and mentoring opportunities to establishing clear lines of communication and providing regular feedback.

By the end of this section, you should understand the following key points, and be able to use them in the management of your marketing group:

- How to clearly define roles, set expectations and measure performance outcomes for employees
- The importance of identifying a path for individual professional development and personal growth within the organization
- How to establish and maintain clear communications and feedback within the group

1.1   Define Roles, Job Descriptions, and Expectations

Before any A/E/C marketing team can thrive, it must function efficiently. In this world of unanticipated fire drills, unrealistic deadlines and unusual requests, it's important for the marketing team to be in top shape. Everyone on the team must be flexible and should know their role, and job descriptions and titles should be clearly understood.

If you were to ask a team of marketers to define the specific role of a team member based on their daily tasks, you may find that very different titles are used for essentially

the same role. In firms where this is the case, confusion over role definitions can create internal problems when it comes to salary reviews or transitions from one division to another. You must agree upon a set of fundamental job descriptions for all marketing staff. This is the foundation for building a powerful team.

Now that you have a goal in mind, what shape do you want this team to take? Does a marketing team resemble a pit crew on a race track, where each individual has a specific task for which they are responsible? Or perhaps a surgical team in an operating room, where the team performs multiple and various functions under the direction of a skilled leader? The organization of the team should be outlined to keep roles clearly defined and lines of communication open. Most effective marketing teams are made up of individuals from both the technical and non-technical pool.

Probably the most familiar model in the A/E/C industry is that of the seller-doer. In this model, a technical professional may or may not have the responsibility of finding leads and initiating contact, but they are responsible for leading the charge during the pursuit of a project, where their technical expertise and interaction with the client will help close the deal. This model represents the natural progression that emerges from a small firm structure, where one or two owners are responsible for selling the firm's expertise to its clients.

In larger firms, this model has been strengthened by the evolution of professional service marketers, whose skills in marketing and BD can free the seller-doer from the time-consuming tasks of identifying and qualifying leads, allowing them to concentrate on maintaining existing client relationships until their efforts are needed to woo a new client who has been carefully prepped by the marketing professional. This model leverages the most meaningful relationships among the client, technical staff and marketing professional. Use this model to determine the right mix for your firm, depending on its size and future growth expectations.

Often in a smaller firm, one marketing professional will perform multiple roles as outlined below. The size of the firm will typically dictate how many of the non-technical positions are necessary. Generally, a firm of approximately 20 personnel would be ready for a marketing team. Until firms reach this size, most rely on the owner or principal of the firm to perform BD and marketing functions. Once the firm passes this threshold, additional personnel are necessary to support the BD function of the principal(s).

To fully explore what scenarios might make sense, it would be helpful to review the responsibilities of the various technical and marketing professionals who can compose your team. We'll discuss later how these roles may change or overlap depending on the size of the firm.

The following definitions should clarify the role and expectations of each team member by title:

- **Principal closer.** This individual, generally a registered professional, focuses the majority of his or her time on marketing. Typically an owner or senior-level partner of the firm, this individual has the ability to sign contracts and commit resources to clients.

- **Seller-doer.** While also a senior-level registered professional, this person splits time between project work and marketing. The majority of time is focused on selling projects, with a lesser percentage spent on actual billable work. This individual may also have authority to sign contracts in certain situations.

- **Doer-closer.** The focus for this individual is on marketing existing clients, with 80 percent or more of their time spent on actual billable projects. Roughly half are registered, and they are most often found in the role of project manager or other senior positions within the firm. They may not have ownership or partnership in the firm.

- **Principal-in-charge of marketing.** The principal-in-charge has absolute authority on marketing issues within the framework of normal operations and delegates the day-to-day responsibility for the marketing program and activities to lower levels of management. This individual is a firm owner or member of the highest level of firm management.

- **Chief marketing officer.** This individual is responsible for the overall direction of the firm with respect to strategic growth, market planning, budgeting and staffing. They are familiar with trends, growth industries and best practices. The ability to build relationships across the organization and collaborate with all team members is essential. This individual should have an executive role in the company, often as vice president or principal. In smaller firms, these duties will be performed by a principal.

- **BD director.** The BD director is responsible for representing the firm at the highest level to clients, peer organizations and business associates. They organize, plan, schedule and manage the firm's sales efforts. In larger firms, this will be a member of firm management, typically one who holds at least an associate-level position and often is a vice president or principal. In smaller firms, these duties will be performed by a principal.

- **Marketing director.** The director represents the firm to clients, peer organizations and business associations. This individual establishes marketing policies and procedures and determines marketing objectives to meet firm-wide goals. They should have a thorough understanding of the A/E/C industry terminology and procedures and excellent leadership/managerial and mentoring/teaching skills.

- **BD manager.** The BD manager seeks business opportunities for the firm, which could be market-specific depending on the firm's size. They schedule meetings with new/existing clients to discover project information and work with technical staff to develop proposals and scopes of work and estimate fees. In larger firms, this may be a member of firm management, often at the associate level. In smaller firms, these duties may be performed by a principal.

- **Marketing manager.** Responsible for the implementation of the marketing plan and overall marketing efforts, this individual develops internal resources and collateral and is often responsible for tracking sales and budgets. A strong knowledge about all aspects of the marketing process is required. In larger firms, this may be a member of firm management, often at the associate level. In smaller firms, these duties may be performed by the office manager or principal.

- **Marketing coordinator.** The coordinator is responsible for proposal content and presentation materials. Strong writing, communication, organizational and time-management skills are imperative, as they coordinate all members of the pursuit team—both internal and external. These individuals are the ultimate multi-taskers. They can be new to the A/E/C industry as long as they have the essential traits mentioned above. In smaller firms, this may be the only professional marketer on staff.

- **Marketing assistant.** This individual provides support to the marketing team with a variety of tasks that can include clerical work, collating proposals and qualification brochures, printing presentation materials, updating marketing support materials and assisting where needed. In smaller firms, this may be a receptionist or administrative person, assisting firm principals in their efforts.

For a more detailed list of the responsibilities, skill sets and education/certification requirements associated with each position, see SMPS Blueprints in the Related Resources section.

1.1.1   Structure Your Department

Most A/E/C firms have less than 50 employees. There are smaller firms that are on an expansion track, while others are contracting. No matter in which direction your firm is headed, growing pains in the marketing department abound. Ambitious small firms can ache just as much from too few marketers as the constricting mid-sized firm may suffer from too many. Consider the following as a guide for how to structure your marketing department, based on the size of your firm.

- **Fewer than 20 employees.** The principal of a firm with less than 20 employees is generally very close to clients. The majority of the work comes from word-of-mouth and personal contacts. With only one or two closers necessary to support a firm of this size, there is minimal need for a structured marketing department. When a firm reaches roughly 20 employees, there is value in adding a marketing coordinator to facilitate production of proposals and preparation of presentation materials.

- **Small firm (20-50 employees).** A firm of this size has the capacity to perform on larger projects and can begin to target specific markets. A marketing plan should be in place to guide the decisions of two to three principals who will lead BD efforts. A senior marketing coordinator or marketing manager who can perform all marketing functions is critical. As the firm becomes more diversified, public relations and sales needs increase. The team will require a marketing assistant or an additional coordinator as the firm becomes more sophisticated in its marketing approach.

- **Mid-sized and growing (50-100 employees).** If a firm is growing or in the mid-range, there are additional requirements of the marketing team. Multiple closers, seller-doers and doer-closers are involved in the marketing effort. Generally, one principal takes on overall responsibility for marketing efforts and a formalized marketing plan is in place. Often a marketing director or manager runs the day-to-day operation and, working with the marketing principal, is ultimately responsible for making go/no-go decisions, directing the marketing team and achieving sales goals. Additionally, a marketing manager, several coordinators and possibly an assistant are necessary.

- **Large and diverse (100+ employees).** In a large, multi-layered firm, the marketing team becomes a central force within the firm and often includes a director, business developer, manager, coordinators, graphic designers, public relations personnel, database administrator and marketing assistant. Generally, these firms have formed internal studio groups of specialists in niche markets or services. Each of these studios could have different marketing needs. Additionally, regional or branch offices may also be a consideration. To avoid any kind of divergence (of the brand or goals), these firms must have one person in charge of marketing, who may or may not be a principal in the firm. Several marketing teams may be needed to address the needs of various studios.

- **In the case of a firm specializing in a niche market, a principal leader who is entrenched in the marketplace is essential.** This individual is seen as an industry expert, often speaking at conferences, writing white papers and advising clients. Niche market firms can truly benefit from the addition of a market researcher and a strong writer to support their activities.

- **Full-service firm (100+ employees).** Full-service large firms are major players in the national, and often international, market. With multiple branch or regional operations, they have sophisticated and elaborate marketing teams. It is imperative that these firms continue to win a stream of projects to keep a healthy backlog. The only way to win work at this pace is with a stout team of marketing professionals. A full-service firm requires a full-force marketing team: chief marketing officer, marketing director, business developer, marketing manager, public relations/communications manager, marketing coordinators, graphic designers and marketing assistants.

1.2   Establish Performance Outcomes, Expectations, and Metrics

Use the assessment tool provided in SMPS Blueprints (or a similar one) to measure your staff's knowledge areas and skill sets. Based on the results, develop expectations for each staff person, including the metrics by which they will be evaluated. Each person will have a different set of metrics depending on their skill level, how many years of experience they have, and the responsibilities required for their job. For example, it would be unrealistic to hold an employee in an entry-level position, such as a marketing assistant, to the metrics of a marketing manager who has 10 years of experience. Communicate these expectations and metrics clearly with each person.

Although the skills needed for each role will vary widely, there are some specific skills that should be present in all marketing professionals:

- **Writing.** This skill is often what the A/E/C technical professional lacks.
- **Ability to multi-task.** If this skill is not mastered, the marketing professional is doomed to failure.
- **Team player.** A history of working with others in a similar role demonstrates an ability to step up when needed and share the load when necessary.
- **Personal interest.** The best marketing professionals have some hint of passion for the industry they serve.

1.3   Identify Training and Professional Development Needs

Another important task is the training and mentoring of marketing staff. This serves to raise the self-esteem of the marketers, which in turn elevates the marketing effort of a firm. Work with the human resources (HR) department to encourage and support the marketing staff by developing a Professional Development Plan (PDP). (A sample PDP is provided in section 1.6.) For example, promote continuing education through professional organizations, such as SMPS. This organization has a certification program that tests the mastery of the Domains of Practice for the industry. Encourage the marketing staff to become certified. Ultimately, you will have a knowledgeable team that will catapult your marketing efforts to new heights.

We will discuss how to identify training needs and develop a training program to greater depth in section 4.

1.4   Provide Mentoring and Coaching Opportunities

The difference between mentoring and coaching may not seem immediately apparent, but they are, in fact, distinct. Mentoring is the long-term development of a professional relationship between two people that fosters trust, confidence and mutual learning. The relationship might originally focus on specific skills that the mentee wants to develop or issues they want advice for, but eventually it becomes more about helping the mentee navigate along in their career, beyond anything directly related to their current position. These might include personal concerns, such as the development of a good work/life balance or self-confidence.

Coaching is short-term, ending when the student demonstrates that they have sufficiently improved in a particular skill. The goal of this relationship is to improve the student's performance in a concrete issue or skill set, such as public speaking, time management or strategic thinking.

Put another way, mentoring is about the relationship, while coaching is about the task. For more information on the difference between mentoring and coaching, see Related Resources.

1.4.1   Mentoring

A new pattern of mentoring has emerged in recent years, where the mentee creates agendas and drives the direction of the process. Modern-day mentoring offers more of an information exchange, where mentees—whether on staff or in regional offices around the world—can offer value in exchange for the guidance they receive. A common example of "reverse mentoring" is when a mentee from the Millennial Generation coaches an executive about social media in return for wisdom about how to get ahead in the company. In this way, wisdom is not passed only from teacher to student, but discovered together through a learning relationship.

IDEA

Ask your mentor/mentee what they're reading these days, which can open doors to great discussion and provide meaningful insights into their mindset.

Having a mentor can be one of the most powerful influences in a person's life. As such, firm leaders should help their staff to find a mentor, especially newer staff members who don't yet know how to find the qualified pool of people out there to whom they could reach out. Ideally, everyone on staff would have someone they could turn to for advice, problem-solving, and encouragement—whether that person was in the same firm or industry, or from a different business area.

Of course, it's not the case that everyone finds a mentor right away. The job of the leader is more to make their staff aware of opportunities that might make it easier to find someone themselves. For example, many SMPS chapters have developed a mentor/protégé program where young SMPS members are matched up with more senior staff. One such program, called One2One, is described in the story below.

TARGET POINT

One2One

Mentoring relationships begin in many different ways and are often very organic in nature. In the SMPS Colorado program One2One, this wasn't the case. Pairings were made after a speed dating-like session where mentors and protégés decided who would be a good fit for them.

Jennifer Van Vleet, CPSM, a 15-year industry veteran who has held various positions at two different engineering companies, was paired with Laura Schindler, CPSM, now in the sixth year of her first marketing role in an engineering firm that doesn't have any senior marketers.

Initially, Van Vleet and Schindler didn't really know how they would match up—in personality, approach or expectations. This is one of the inherent challenges in being assigned to a pair in such a formal way, as it takes time to build trust and enter into meaningful dialogue.

The One2One program scheduled monthly group meetings to explore growth areas and topics. This gave pairs something to discuss at one-on-one meetings and helped them learn about each other more quickly.

As they discovered, a lot can be learned through intentional conversation and dedicating time to their personal and professional growth. The formal mentoring plan defined a clear schedule and expectation for their meetings, effectively setting aside time at least twice a month to really reflect on career and personal goals. It was definitely challenging to find time consistently, but as Schindler says, "For me, that kind of reflection time is vital to keeping me motivated."

Being paired with someone outside their own organizations was one of the best things about the program. For Schindler, as in many firms, there were no senior-level marketing staff from whom she could learn. Having an outside perspective, especially from someone who had been in a similar situation, was a great inspiration and resource.

"I think it was helpful that Jen didn't know the people involved in the ins and outs of my company's culture," Schindler said. "Her reactions and ideas were more objective and strategy-driven that those from within my firm would be."

Both Van Vleet and Schindler found that the sharing of ideas, coaching, learning and self-reflection all came into play, and that the results could be different for the mentor and protégé.

Van Vleet found that some of the challenges faced earlier in her career had actually reappeared in her new company. "Working with Laura gave me the opportunity to not only think through what she was doing, but also to examine concepts and efforts that helped me to solve my own challenge."

For Schindler, meeting with Van Vleet helped her step back from daily activities and approach her career more strategically. "This has really created more purpose and accountability in how I approach my job. In addition to being a resource for examples and materials, talking with Jen keeps my ideas and plans in perspective."

> **Key Concepts for this Story:**
> - Taking time to connect with others in your industry in an individual way is a great way to participate in the growth of your field
> - Engaging in dialogue with others opens up perspectives and ways of thinking to problem solve
> - Being involved in a mentoring program will benefit both the mentor and the protégé

1.4.2   Coaching

While mentoring is fairly unstructured, coaching requires clearly defined goals and a plan for how the coach will help the student achieve those goals. Effective leaders will ensure that all key staff members have access to a coach's support.

The coaching process needs to be supported by a solid framework, bolstered by clear objectives. Those objectives might include the following:

- Providing an honest (but tactful) evaluation of the student's performance
- Teaching specific knowledge or skill sets
- Improvements in behavior
- Nurturing intrinsic motivation
- Encouraging dedication and persistence
- Promoting independence

1.5   Have Regular Team Meetings

One of the critical skills that all marketing professionals must have is the ability to communicate. This transcends everything you submit to clients, but also must be present in your daily routines. Who hasn't fired off an email they later regretted? Or been confused by a message that was misinterpreted? It's also easier and less invasive to send an email rather than make a few phone calls. However, marketers must find a balance between emails, phone calls and face-to-face meetings.

Creating a culture that relies on email alone is dangerous. Encouraging teams to pick up the phone rather than wait for a reply to an email is often more productive. The information exchange is timelier and more accurate. Often in larger firms, the marketing team is not physically located in the vicinity of the technical staff. If the marketing team is not colocated with the technical staff, it is even more important to get up and walk around the office. The more a marketing professional is woven into the technical staff, the more they learn about current and upcoming projects and events. It also provides visibility so that technical personnel can understand the benefit marketing brings to the accomplishments of the firm.

Working with multiple office locations presents specific challenges for communication. The key is to have enough "face time" to engage the team. It's also important that everyone remember that we are all human. Things run much more smoothly when

you're able to spend time with people. While it is not always possible to work across the desk, the marketing professional must devise proactive strategies and find a balance between modes of communication.

Conduct regular meetings—either in person or via video conference—to provide the face-to-face interaction that is so important. The frequency of these meetings will vary depending on the size and location of your staff. For example, if your firm has multiple offices, each office might have weekly meetings with their own teams to make sure that they understand their objectives and goals for that week. Then they might all call in for an inter-office video conference once per month to report on their activities for that month and confirm a plan for the next.

TARGET POINT

Communication with virtual or remote staff should occur just as frequently as with in-house staff. Without the ability to drop by each other's offices with a question, or to bond during a coffee break, it takes a concerted effort to ensure that a virtual staff member still feels like a part of the team. And remember that not all modes of communication are of equal value. Video calls are far superior to phone calls, as facial expressions and body language often speak louder than words.

One of the many benefits of inter-office communication is the ability to identify areas where team members need assistance and provide help. Say your office's small team only includes one person with graphic design experience, and they're feeling overwhelmed by the amount of work they've been entrusted with lately. Identify whether there is someone in another office who has the time and ability to lend a hand. Sharing resources and skills between offices saves money, but, more importantly, it eases the workload of your staff and helps to avoid burnout. But you can't just wait until the last minute to realize your team could use help—tapping into these resources requires good planning and frequent communication. And that's where holding regular team meetings comes into play.

But it can't all be work, work, work—team-building should also be fun. Go out to dinner together when your team is working out of town on a big pursuit. Allow everyone the chance to decompress after a whirlwind of activity. Depending on the team members' personalities, that may mean a happy hour, sporting event, or some other non-work-related activity. An annual conference or summit for the marketing team is also an opportunity to build camaraderie. The team that plays together, stays together.

1.6   Help Staff Create a Professional Development Plan (PDP)

During your annual evaluation meetings with staff, work with them to create a PDP that documents their plans for personal development over the next few years. This can include plans related to their career, education (e.g., to attain a certification), relationships (e.g., to find a mentor), or self-improvement. It should include a clear picture of where they will be in three to five years if they have succeeded in meeting their goals; a specific skill they want to develop, and what mastering that skill would look like; and the steps they will complete in order to achieve their goals. It may also include a statement of their career/lifestyle priorities, an analysis of the risks, and a plan B.

Make sure that the goals they outline are achievable. Achievable goals have certain characteristics, and a good way to remember these is with the acronym SMART:

- **Specific.** Not "do good marketing." Who can tell what that entails?
- **Measurable.** Not "increase my proposal hit rate," but "achieve a 40% proposal hit rate."
- **Attainable.** Goals must be attainable, or you'll be disappointed and demoralized.
- **Relevant.** Alignment with other goals is important. Does this goal help your firm move forward?
- **Time-bound.** Goals are more likely to be met if they have a deadline.

Below is a sample PDP template.

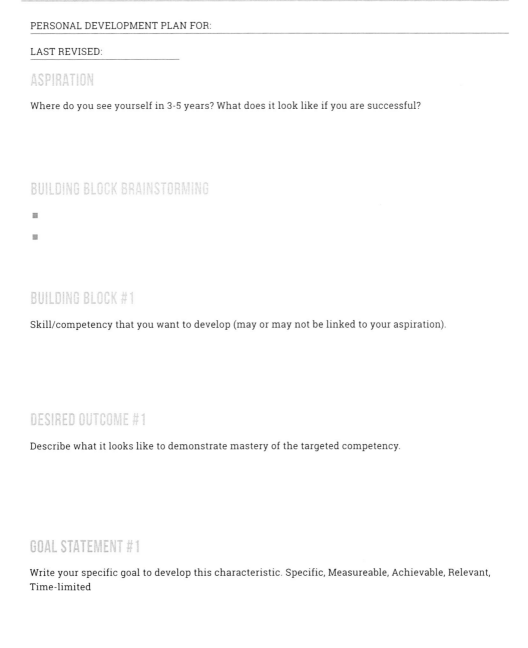

PERSONAL DEVELOPMENT PLAN

PERSONAL DEVELOPMENT PLAN FOR:

LAST REVISED:

ASPIRATION

Where do you see yourself in 3-5 years? What does it look like if you are successful?

BUILDING BLOCK BRAINSTORMING

-
-

BUILDING BLOCK #1

Skill/competency that you want to develop (may or may not be linked to your aspiration).

DESIRED OUTCOME #1

Describe what it looks like to demonstrate mastery of the targeted competency.

GOAL STATEMENT #1

Write your specific goal to develop this characteristic. Specific, Measureable, Achievable, Relevant, Time-limited

Figure 1.1 - Sample Professional Development Plan (provided by Mark Tawara)

1.7   Conduct Performance Evaluations

It is important to conduct regular, ongoing assessments of your personnel—annual evaluations are necessary, too, but not enough. Monthly, bi-monthly or quarterly discussions will prevent surprises at the annual evaluation. Communicate with your staff often to tell them how they're doing. These discussions don't have to be called "evaluations"; they can be informal monthly check-ins. Ask your staff: "How are things going? What concerns do you have? How are you managing your workload?" Also take this opportunity to bring up issues: "I noticed you're having challenges on this project or with this manager. Tell me about what you're experiencing and how I can help you overcome those challenges." Address issues as they arise, rather than saving them all for an overwhelming end-of-the-year rundown.

The goal is that when the annual evaluation rolls around, there shouldn't be any surprises for you or your staff—everything should have been discussed over the course of the year. The annual performance evaluations are, therefore, simply a formal writeup of what you both already know. Apart from that, use these meetings to focus on your staff's PDP and SMART goals. Establish PDPs and goals for the next year (or longer) and discuss how they've done on these measures over the past year. You could even conduct this kind of evaluation twice a year. An example schedule might look like this: In January, you meet with each staff member to set goals specifying what they want to accomplish over the next year. In July, you meet again to see how they're progressing. Are their goals still realistic? Do they want to change any of their goals? What can each of you do to ensure that the remaining goals are accomplished by the end of the year?

This combination of frequent, informal check-ins punctuated by annual (or bi-annual) formal evaluations and goal-setting will go far to keep lines of communication open and make sure that everyone is on the same page. Let your staff members know how they're doing, and tell them often.

 1.8 Key Terms

Below are the main terms covered in this section:

- Seller-doer
- Doer-closer
- Mentor
- Coach
- Personal Development Plan (PDP)
- SMART goals

2   Develop an Internal Marketing Communications Program

What goes on within your marketing department should be of interest to the organization as a whole, and vice versa. Using the sales pipeline to keep everyone updated on wins, losses and proposal generation will let the company know how your group is doing, and identifying leads early can mean all the difference in seeing and acting on a lucrative business opportunity.

By the end of this section, you should understand the following key points, and be able to use them in the management of your marketing group:

- Understand that the pipeline report is a resource for keeping track of leads and monitoring progress, while providing a focus for stakeholder involvement in the sales process

- How to use industry events as a source for generating leads

- The importance of keeping everyone up-to-date on new opportunities and capabilities across the organization, to promote cross-sell and up-sell opportunities

2.1   Track and Communicate Relevant Information

The entire firm should be kept up-to-date on your company's marketing performance data and BD opportunities and outcomes. Keep track of the firm's wins, losses, monthly proposal numbers, outstanding requests for proposals (RFPs) and other marketing performance data, and communicate that information frequently with the entire team. BD activities to be tracked include leads, client meetings, presentations, new leads and activities on existing leads. This information can be shared in many different ways—through a weekly email, for instance, or at monthly staff meetings—but the important point is that you do it.

But before we get into the various methods of tracking and sharing this information, we must define exactly what we mean by a "lead."

Too many business developers believe that a lead is a call from a colleague about a potential project or an article in the newspaper about an upcoming project. While this is true, it misses the mark. Timing is critical (or fatal) in leads. Being the first person to contact a prospect can create a decided advantage for your firm, an advantage your competitors may not be able to overcome. A better way to describe a lead is as "an indication or a clue."

A potential lead could be indicated by any number of things, including:

- A change in codes or regulations that will produce new areas for work (ADA, IAQ, LEED, NFPA, NEC, and EPA Safe Drinking Water Rules are some examples)

- Development of a piece of property next door to an undeveloped piece owned by one of your clients

- Extension of water/sewer service into a new area
- Adoption of a new municipal thoroughfare plan
- Hiring of a key individual by a university
- Announcement of a new employer in an area
- Drought conditions in an area
- Businesses that refinance/consolidate existing debt
- Market sector growth/consolidation
- Proposed bond issues for construction

The point is that changes in any business, institution or local business environment can generally be seen as a lead in retrospect. In order to be most effective, you must always keep your eyes and ears open. The earlier you catch on to a lead, the better.

We'll discuss more about how to create a lead tracking system in section 3.

2.1.1   Pipeline Report

Developing and using a sales pipeline report can help you track your progress, build accountability into BD and increase your sales revenue. While some firms understand the importance of measuring the amount of new business opportunity in their sales pipeline, many lack the ability to use the pipeline effectively to reach their growth goals.

Depending on how your firm is organized for growth, the sales pipeline can be used for the firm as a whole, a business unit or niche team, individuals or all of the above. The pipeline report tracks whether you have enough activity, whether you're focused on the right activities and whether potential sales opportunities are being moved through the sales cycle. It also measures your close rate on proposals.

Creating a pipeline report doesn't have to involve a complicated reporting system. In fact, a Microsoft Excel spreadsheet with a variety of "sorts" can be very effective. Your partners and staff are likely familiar with Microsoft Excel and won't have to learn a new system, which increases the chances that they will actually use the report. The following table is an example of a simple, yet effective pipeline report.

PIPELINE REPORT - FOR A TEAM OR AN INDIVIDUAL

Target Company	Lead Originator	Working Lead	Date Originated	Client/ Prospect	Business Unit/Niche	Service	Idea	Made Contact	Proposal	Close Probability	Pipeline
Company 1	Partner A	Partner A	1-15-08	Client	Health Care	Tax Consulting	$4,000			5%	$200
Company 2	Partner B	Partner B	12-12-07	Client	Construction	Cost Seg			$5,000	50%	$2,500
Company 3	Partner C	Partner C	3-4-07	Prospect	Higher Education	Audit		$10,000		25%	$2,500
Company 4	Partner D	Partner D	4-12-08	Client	Mfg.	Bus Val	$5,000			5%	$250
Company 5	Partner A	Partner B	11-29-07	Prospect	Construction	Cost Seg	$8,000			5%	$400
Company 6	Partner B	Partner D	1-7-08	Client	Mfg.	Succession Plng	$3,500			5%	$175
Company 7	Partner C	Partner B	3-15-08	Client	Mfg.	R&D Study		$25,000		15%	$3,750
Company 8	Partner D	Partner B	2-12-08	Client	Construction	Cost Seg	$7,500			5%	$375
Company 9	Partner A	Partner A	10-4-07	Prospect	Real Estate	Tax Compliance			$4,000	75%	$3,000
Company 10	Partner B	Partner C	2-23-08	Client	NFP	40100 Admin		$3,000		20%	$600
TOTAL PIPELINE											**$13,750**
GROWTH GOAL											**$50,000**
PERCENTAGE OF GOAL											**27.5%**

Sample Pipeline Report (Marketing Handbook)

This table shows the information you should track for each sales opportunity. Let's take a closer look at the important sections of a pipeline report.

- **Lead originator.** The sales manager of a firm or the BD team leader should monitor how many new business opportunities each team member is bringing to the firm. This is how you can assess the effectiveness of their BD activity and determine if the firm is getting a positive return on investment (ROI) on the time invested. Lead originators may bring new leads to the firm through referrals, existing relationships, prospecting or other BD activities. Lead originators may also bring opportunities to the firm simply by being well-positioned in the community or industry they serve. Anyone in the firm can be a lead originator.

- **Working lead.** This should be the person who will lead the follow-up activity for each opportunity. This person may or may not be the same person who originated the lead. It should be the person with the best skills and aptitude to move the opportunity through the sales cycle. The lead sales person should be focused on the industry of the target company and/or have the service expertise that matches the target company's initial need. A pipeline report can help your firm set realistic goals for lead sales professionals and hold them accountable for their efforts.

- **Client/prospect.** The pipeline report should be used to monitor sales to both repeat and prospective clients. Experience demonstrates that there is typically as much growth opportunity within the existing client base as there is with new client relationships. Measurement and accountability are necessary to make sure that you are being proactive about pursuing new projects with your former clients. If you're not proactively meeting the needs of your existing clients, you also leave them vulnerable to your competitors attempting to serve their needs. If your firm is multi-disciplinary (architecture, engineering and/or construction), you might have an opportunity to extend your current projects beyond their original scope.

- **Business unit or niche.** It is helpful to know what industry niche or business unit the potential new work will be associated with so you can track how you're going to reach your growth goals for each area.

- **Service.** This information can be helpful during discussions of the pipeline report to determine who can help with sales efforts, as well as for tracking whether you're working a balance of opportunities.

- **Amount.** Don't let the difficulty of estimating the fee cause you to give up on the report—at this point, a rough approximation of what the prospect or client might need based on initial thoughts or conversations is enough. This amount goes in the "idea" column if you haven't had any conversations with the target yet but you think this is a potential opportunity; it goes in the "made contact" column if you've started conversations and plan to follow up; and it goes in the "proposal" column if the client/prospect is interested and has asked for a fee estimate or a formal proposal.

- **Probability of close.** This is also a rough estimate. At the idea stage, it probably shouldn't be any higher than 10 percent. After one or more conversations, you'll have a feel for the probability that this will eventually become closed new business—at this point, it should be somewhere between 25 and 75 percent to stay on the report. Once a proposal or fee is submitted, the probability should be 50 percent or higher.

- **Pipeline.** The pipeline amount is calculated by multiplying the value of the engagement by the probability of close. As you move opportunities from the idea phase to proposal, which increases the probability of closing, the pipeline amount will increase.

2.1.2 Track Upcoming Industry Events

Subscribe to an email list of professional organizations you would like to target for attendance, and forward relevant events to your staff. Also develop a list of conferences to be tracked, along with calls for papers (and their due dates), conference dates, who will be attending, etc. Establish a company calendar populated with these outside events and encourage your staff to sign up to attend a conference, talk, networking opportunity, etc., that they find interesting. At meetings, report on which events have been covered, and which events are targeted for coverage and still need a volunteer attendee. Also bring any upcoming calls for papers or presentations to the group's attention and discuss whether or not to pursue them.

IDEA

Assign one person the responsibility of registering staff for events and updating the calendar. Having a single contact for all employees will make it easier to coordinate— you don't want too many people signing up for one event, or for an important talk to be completely missed.

Create a forum for your employees to share the knowledge they've gained at these events with the rest of the staff. The Hnedak Bobo Group hosts a firm-wide "coffee talk" series that meets once per month for this exact purpose. Staff members use this open platform to share what they've learned since the last meeting, such as marketing tips and techniques picked up at a recent conference. The beauty of this inclusive forum is that it encourages deeper involvement in marketing and BD across all levels of the organization. But there are many other forms that your information sharing program could take.

JDB Engineering, Inc. opts for a more formal approach. Knowledge is shared in company meetings with all staff present, though the duration is usually only 5 or 10 minutes. When Scott Butcher attended Build Business 2010, he came back with a ton of knowledge about social media, which he presented to staff at a company meeting. He then followed up with an hour-long seminar, "Social Media in the A/E/C Industry," and has since implemented Business Development University and updates the content monthly.

However you run these short "seminars," it's a good idea to record the presentations and post them to the firm's Intranet, along with the PDFs of any related Microsoft PowerPoint slides. This way the information is still available for any staff who could not attend or for those who want to go back and reference it later. You should also email summaries of conferences, trade shows, networking events and professional organization meetings to your staff to quickly distribute noteworthy information.

2.2   Establish Regular Meetings with Stakeholders

Schedule regular meetings with senior staff, project managers and any other necessary stakeholders to discuss your firm's marketing and BD outcomes and performance. Set it up for a time when you can be sure that everyone you need to participate will be in the office and free from any other mandatory obligations. Establish attendance requirements and have managers communicate these requirements to their staff.

Don't forget to invite a stakeholder whose insight is essential to the project—make a list!

2.2.1   Create an Agenda

Prior to holding the meeting, define what you want to accomplish. Do this well before the day of the meeting—if everyone shows up without knowing what they're working toward, what's the point of meeting at all? In the week before the session, set up short interviews with the participants in order to come up with a list of desired outcomes. Here are some questions to get the conversation started:

- What items must be discussed during this session?
- At the end of the dialogue, what does success look like?
- What main points should be addressed in a new marketing/BD plan?
- What are the most likely challenges we'll face in attaining these goals?

The answers to these questions will give you valuable insight into the direction the session should take and the expectations of the participants. Consolidate responses into a single document—the agenda. Send this out before the meeting. At the beginning of the session, have the key person (who may be you!) talk once again about the desired outcomes.

These pre-meeting interviews should provide you with a good agenda, as well as an idea of which points should be given priority. Certainly focus on those, but be flexible. It's important to be able to tweak the agenda as the discussion calls for it—depending on the situation, you may need to adjust the flow or timing when items are brought up, increase the pace, or even delete a specific agenda item. Rather than plodding through the agenda point by point, connect the dots of the conversation and see where it leads. At the same time, be sure all items are eventually addressed (or consciously deleted). Don't get stuck circling around one point to the neglect of the others. This is often a difficult thing to do as conflict arises (as it invariably will), which is why your role as a facilitator is so important. (For more information on facilitation tips and managing conflict, see Domain 2.)

Having a good agenda will help you meet one of the golden rules of meetings: start and end on time. This may sound simple, but you've probably already noticed how rare it is for a meeting to start the minute it's supposed to and not run over. Be precise about when the session will start, stick to that, and keep track of the time so you know when to wrap one discussion up and move on to the next. Leave around 10-15 minutes at the end free so you don't feel rushed during the debrief and assignment of action items.

2.2.2   Distribute a Detailed Report

Prior to holding the meeting, a detailed report of all relevant data should be distributed to attendees. It's important that your firm's sales manager or BD manager use the pipeline report we discussed above at monthly sales meetings. The team should spend time reviewing actual sales results, the pipeline report and BD activities.

Hafer Associates, an Evansville, IN-based architectural, engineering, planning, and interior design firm with six principals and more than 35 employees, has a history of aggressively using its pipeline report to guide BD activities.

The pipeline is now deeply imbedded in the firm's day-to-day culture. "We review our pipeline report every two weeks in a marketing meeting with principals and associates," says Hafer Marketing Coordinator Jill Harpole. "Everyone is expected to update the report before the meeting, and the report leads our entire discussion."

Most principals understand the importance of continuous BD. In fact, a majority of them can immediately identify prospects in their market. However, understanding the value doesn't guarantee action. While some firms may not incorporate the process to the degree Hafer has, a clear pipeline report helps principals focus their efforts on maintaining prospect/client contact. "We're always trying to advance our relationships and increase the probability of winning a project," explains Harpole. "The report is a great way to measure our current status with each client/prospect and identify what steps we need to take to improve it."

The pipeline report is a straightforward, effective tool to help you track activity, hold your team accountable and ultimately help you reach your annual growth goals. It will likely take a while to get your team familiar with and accustomed to using the pipeline report. But it shouldn't take long to start seeing some of the benefits. Discussing pipeline reports on a regular basis will show team members exactly what is expected of them.

Firms should consider the following questions when viewing the report:

- **"Is there enough in the pipeline?"** In order to have a reasonably good chance of meeting your growth goal, your firm should have the equivalent of your annual growth goal in the pipeline on an ongoing basis. When you're first starting out with the report, it can take up to six months to ramp up, but your ongoing target should be the equivalent of your annual growth goal.

- **"Are we working the client and prospect opportunities?"** When you set growth goals, know how much of your growth opportunity is with former and existing clients and how much needs to come from acquiring new clients; the more specific your growth goals are, the better chance you have of reaching them. Sort your pipeline report by client vs. prospect opportunities and assess how you're progressing regarding each goal. This will help you determine whether you're doing the right activities. If you're not, it will illustrate whether you need to engage in more prospecting activity (e.g., asking for referrals, networking with industry groups or doing direct marketing) or have more conversations with existing clients about expanded services and touch base with past clients regarding future opportunities.

- **"Are we moving opportunities from the idea stage to proposal?"** Each month when you review the report, make sure that the items that were in the idea stage last month have moved forward or been removed from the report. If the same items are sitting in the idea column, this means you aren't working the sales cycle. The pipeline report can be a useful tool to help your people decide how to spend their BD time—if you have 30 minutes per day to devote to BD, pull out the report and figure out who you can call to advance a sales opportunity through the sales cycle. Information in the pipeline report might indicate a need for training—if you're not moving targets from the "interested" phase to proposals and closes, it might mean your firm needs help developing essential sales skills such as creating urgency, communicating value and/or responding to sales objections.

- **"Is our close rate on proposals sufficient?"** As you review the pipeline report each month, you'll start to get a feel for how many of your opportunities that reach the proposal stage (whether it's a formal proposal or simply a submitted fee for a project) actually become new business. You should aim to close, or achieve a service agreement with, at least half of these opportunities. You can even add columns for closed work and lost work and track it on the same report. Once an engagement has been decided, whether won or lost, it should be removed from the pipeline.

TARGET POINT
Remember to tie the pipeline report back to individual, team and firm goals. Everything you talk about at your meetings should align with the goals and initiatives developed in your firm's marketing and strategic plans.

Firms can use a pipeline report to track their progress on many different levels. It's a key tool to track growth activities by partner, by niche, by recurring work and by special projects. It also makes it easy to track new client activities vs existing client activities and is a constant reminder of where a firm needs to add more activity.

Using the different fields you enter into the report, you can sort and subtotal in a variety of ways to determine your progress towards BD goals:

- **Sort by lead originator.** Are partners generating enough new business opportunity for the firm? This can be an indication of whether partners are working effective referral source relationships and/or asking clients for referrals.

- **Sort by working lead.** Are those who are skilled and willing to work the sales cycle doing sales follow up? How many items does each partner have in the idea or contact stage vs those they've moved to proposal?

- **Sort by business unit or industry niche.** If you've set separate goals for departments or teams, you can use the pipeline report for each group to evaluate how they're tracking towards meeting their goal.

2.3 Create Awareness of Company's Services/Offerings for Cross-Selling

A firm's exposure to, contact with and potential influence over the client during a project provides an excellent opportunity to reinforce the firm's full range of experience and capabilities. Every member of the firm is responsible for having a basic understanding of the firm's complete range of services and capabilities and to be able to explain them, at least broadly, to clients and colleagues when successful stealth marketing/BD presents an opportunity.

Prior to venturing out to meet and greet potential clients and search for new opportunities, business developers must educate themselves about the firm's internal

business aspects. This includes understanding and clearly articulating the services the firm offers, being knowledgeable about the firm's resources, knowing about project execution and understanding the financial aspects of the business. Identify best ways of communicating, developing and mastering the various ways of relationship building, connect the BD effort to the development of proposals and presentations and cultivate a client maintenance system.

Develop regular staff training sessions where staff from different departments present on the services offered by your firm, new technologies they're working with and share their knowledge with the rest of the staff. These could be in the form of "lunch and learns," after hours or any of the ideas we've discussed previously. Every service in the A/E/C industry has its own vocabulary—buzz words, acronyms, hot topics—and these differences in definition and emphasis can easily trip someone up if they don't understand exactly what they mean. For example, PIC may mean "principal in charge" for one group in a firm, while another uses it to refer to the "public improvement commission." Make sure that your staff knows the language used by each service.

Print and online publications are another way you can get this information across to your staff. An internal newsletter, blog or weekly email can provide ample opportunities for knowledge-sharing. An employee publication, for example, can serve your statement of purpose by containing stories about company policies, programs, the services your organization offers its clients and financial information. It can give management a way to foster enthusiasm among employees and to give employees a sense of company pride and ownership by providing information about what is expected of them—and what they can expect from the company.

Once you have decided how often you will publish, stick to your schedule. There's nothing more damaging to your credibility than starting out as a weekly, becoming a monthly, falling off to a quarterly and then to a semi-annual publication. Even if you don't think employees or clients are peeking in their mailboxes wondering why your newsletter isn't there yet, your audience will eventually disregard your publication because they can't count on it. The same rule applies to other mediums—blog posts and lunch and learns are less effective when they're unpredictable.

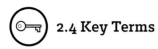 **2.4 Key Terms**

Below are the main terms covered in this section:

- Lead
- Pipeline report
- Lead originator
- Working lead
- Client/prospect (column)
- Business unit/niche (column)
- Service (column)
- Amount (column)
- Idea (column)
- Made contact (column)
- Proposal (column)
- Probability of close
- Pipeline amount
- Cross-selling

3 Develop, Implement, and Maintain Information Management Systems

Effective communication relies on readily available and reliable information, so it is no surprise that marketing effectiveness relies increasingly on various knowledge management systems, in particular the customer (or client) relationship management (CRM) system.

By the end of this section, you should understand the following key points, and be able to use them in the management of your marketing group:

- How to identify and select the CRM system that is right for your organization
- How to develop a workable implementation plan and get company-wide buy-in
- The process of planning, implementing and maintaining the CRM system so that it meets the firm's ongoing needs

3.1 Conduct a Needs Assessment

Knowledge management refers to the process by which organization knowledge is captured, stored, and disseminated within a company. It makes use of the various information systems such as the marketing information system (MIS), the decision support system, the lead tracking system and the CRM system to manage information at a high level, to ensure that it is available to strategic decision-makers and others within the company who could benefit from having access to it. Knowledge management is often under the purview of the company's chief information officer (CIO), who serves as the bridge between the information systems department and the company's top management. We'll talk more specifically about what a CRM system is and how to select one later in this section, but for a more detailed description of the other knowledge management systems, refer to Domain 1.

Software can support and enhance any A/E/C firm's marketing effectiveness. Knowledge management systems are one of the more important software tools at your disposal, as the immediate availability of information saves time and extends the resources of your team. Determining the appropriate software for each management system requires an assessment process to determine the right tool. It also requires a determination of the methodology for the creation, implementation and eventual planned use of the system.

 TARGET POINT
Purchasing any management system just for the sake of having one is a recipe for a disaster. Assess your firm's current and future needs in order to develop a clear purpose for the system. This assessment will help you avoid costly missteps.

The phases of assessment are similar to the strategic planning process that most businesses use. Begin by researching existing conditions:

- What software is currently in place for each information management system?

- Do the original vendors continue to support the systems?

- Are the systems compatible with other systems in use in the business?

- Can the existing systems expand to include input from outside collaborators (e.g., consultants, engineers, suppliers or clients)?

Then, establish clear goals. What is the "vision" or aspiration that your firm has for the system? What purpose will it serve? What processes will it improve?

A needs assessment is a common tool used by design and engineering service providers to measure the effectiveness of their clients' practices. The feedback they gain is used for future planning and in building accountability into their process. The same approach can be applied to finding the right marketing software for your own firm. There are four things that you can do to effectively build more accountability for the implementation of knowledge management software into your organization:

1. Develop consensus on expected outcomes with all primary users

2. Encourage continuous improvement and regularly measure improvements

3. Ensure that all staff (from marketing to principals) participates in the assessment process

4. Take diversity into account; do not mandate one solution for all, but allow for multiple solutions to reach the same goals

Performing an in-depth analysis of the firm's marketing software needs should be part of the larger software program evaluation for your business. A software needs assessment is more effective when the analysis is based on business goals and available resources. Resources include not only existing hardware (e.g., computers) and software, but also the capacity of the infrastructure to support the software and the need for ongoing professional development programs for those who will be using the new systems.

3.2   Select a System

After you have defined your system requirements, you should begin the process of evaluating software based on its function and relative cost. The critical step in minimizing cost is to compare software to your requirements continually, identifying additional features and noting the cost of these extra features. Custom-developed software will produce a program tailored to your exact needs whereas commercial software is generally less expensive and can be implemented more rapidly.

There are three key elements that you need to look for when choosing information management software:

1. **Compatibility.** The system's software should be compatible with your company's other software in order to avoid operating system issues. Consult the vendor and run some tests on your network before purchase.

2. **Availability.** The information in a management system must be available to all users on a real-time basis. This will require you to look at licensing very closely when choosing a platform.

3. **Flexibility.** Every firm is organized and managed differently. Therefore, a management system should be flexible enough to allow users to adapt the information and reporting functions to fit your firm's standard mode of operation.

It is important to ensure that your lead tracking and CRM software has the capability of communicating with your existing accounting and project information systems. The decision of what accounting and project information systems your firm purchases is typically made by the financial and technical staff, so having a good relationship with them helps ensure that marketing and BD staff get a voice in the decision as well.

By integrating your software in this manner you will save tremendous amounts of time with data entry, as existing projects and employees can be automatically associated with relationships in the lead tracking system. This also ensures a greater degree of accuracy in your own system, as accounting systems are known to be extremely precise when compared to other company data systems. Make sure that you know what's going on in the other departments so you aren't stuck with a system you don't want.

3.3   Develop an Implementation Plan

Once it has been determined what software will best serve the marketing effort, the next step is implementation. Successful implementation focuses on people and work processes and uses a strategic, goals-oriented approach. The steps are fairly simple:

1. Define how the system will help your firm improve its effectiveness with clients

2. Determine what impact these strategies will have on information transfer and workflow (internally and externally), and develop a "change management" strategy

3. Implement new work processes to correspond to the new workflow strategy

4. Apply appropriate knowledge management technology to support these work processes (not the other way around)

To ensure success, a knowledge management system needs the support and approval of both management and user groups. Without management support, the system will fail due to lack of credibility; without user support, the system will fail from lack of relevant, accurate data. During the development phase, it is essential to solicit involvement and feedback from both of these groups.

When embarking on a knowledge management program, it is equally important to have the right team involved in the initial analysis, as it is with the final implementation. Typically this will include representatives from marketing, sales, IT and the other divisions of the business that will be affected by the new system. This can and should include project management, design, engineering, finance and procurement. The core team should be kept small and resources brought in as needed and appropriate during the planning and execution phase of the project.

TARGET POINT

Project leadership for the team should come from marketing, preferably the most senior member of the marketing staff. This is a facilitation and organizational (not dictatorial) role, and a keen understanding of team dynamics is important.

Outside consultants can bring added value to the planning for a knowledge management project. They provide a level of objectivity and the ability to provide time resources that may not be available from internal staff. Selecting a consultant should include an analysis of their ability and knowledge of client-centric business planning, change management expertise, business process analysis and design, system architecture and design, and system integration experience. Other skills may include knowledge management technology selection (be wary of potential conflicts of interest with specific vendor partnerships), project management, custom software development and training.

3.3.1   Build Company Buy-In

Probably the most common problem facing corporate knowledge management systems is company-wide buy-in. It's important to build a workforce that sees the value in the management system and wants to utilize it to make their jobs easier. To ensure success, a system needs the support and approval of both management and user groups. By building company-wide buy-in, you will be able to leverage your system as a tool that will help you achieve your strategic goals.

In order to build buy-in, a management system must bring value to all of the user groups. The good news is that, over time, good systems inherently provide value to users. However, the first three to six months of a new system is pivotal to the ultimate success of the system because it generally takes this long to develop the base data that will yield value. Once the base data is established, reporting and clear communication channels provide value to users. Shortening the time it takes to derive value from the system is the first key to building company-wide buy-in. While value will be defined differently for every company—and even for every department and type of system— linking the system to existing data, including, in most cases, accounting systems and client databases, is the most common way to decrease the time it takes for the system to provide value.

Additional ways to build buy-in include:

- Identifying technologically savvy individuals from each user group to lead the implementation effort

- Ensuring that higher-ups review and comment on new data during each of the first 12 weeks so that individuals feel that their efforts are appreciated

- Open communication about the anticipated time that it will take for each user group to begin realizing value from the new system

By establishing your approach for building buy-in early on, you will shorten your timeline to the successful integration of the system and begin the process of changing your corporate culture toward one that embraces knowledge management.

3.4   Develop a Maintenance Plan

A business must maintain current and accurate information in order to have an effective knowledge management system. One person in the firm should take on the responsibility of keeping the marketing information fresh. This can be anyone in the firm who is detail-oriented and persistent. The simplest way to achieve this is by having an information update schedule. Updates can take place bi-monthly, quarterly or bi-annually. Reflect on how often information changes occur within your firm and schedule accordingly. If you are having trouble gathering current information for any system, consider talking with your principals about incorporating the gathering of this information into the annual review process.

When done correctly, this tool can be highly effective. For example, W.S. Bellows Construction Corporation in Houston, Texas completes an annual audit of their marketing information. They identify the information that needs to be updated and take the first quarter of their fiscal year to update all marketing-related information. This exercise keeps their information fresh and accurate.

Creating the most effective knowledge management system for your business is an ongoing effort. As you build and refine your system, you will continually find ways to improve and expand it to increase your firm's effectiveness and success. The exciting thing about a well-run management system is that it can provide you with the statistics and reports that will help you identify ways to make the system more effective and efficient.

To refine your knowledge management system, begin by identifying questions that can help you zero in on both strengths and weaknesses and then look for solutions that can improve your corporate performance. Making the system a consistent part of your company's performance metrics will allow you to understand your lead-to-sales process and provide you with the tools to meet your corporate goals.

3.5   Develop a Customer Relationship Management (CRM) System

A CRM system is just one of the many systems included in a firm's knowledge management program. While similar in purpose to the rest (as a way to collect, maintain and use information), a CRM system is the one marketers are most likely to use on a frequent basis. In this section, we will discuss only the planning, implementation and maintenance of a CRM from an information management perspective. For information on how to use a CRM system as a BD tool, see Domain 3.

CRM is a strategic framework for knowledge management. It works only when processes are implemented that match the business needs to the client's requirements. Look at CRM technologies by asking what they can do from the client's business perspective. The goal of an effective CRM system is to organize internal knowledge history in way that maximizes customer value through simplified—and preferably customized—engagement and transactional processes. It increases profitability by clarifying and defining the effort required to match the client's expectations exactly.

To be effective, a CRM solution needs to engage the client in ways that simplify their interaction with your company, speed up the delivery of services and save them money, all while increasing the service provider's profitability. At the same time, the CRM systems collect, categorize and sort information that will provide the opportunity for increasing value-added services to the same customer, and can facilitate the process of attracting new clients as well.

In some cases, process changes may be necessary to get your technical staff able to provide valuable information. This is one of the key factors that often leads to a perceived failure of the CRM implementation. It is important to have the CRM system make the firm's staff work easier, not harder. If CRM provides value internally, it will be more likely to be utilized as a primary tool for collecting the data needed to increase knowledge. Unfortunately, a study by AMR Research found that, even among top CRM vendors, 47 percent of companies reported serious challenges with end-user adoption.

Knowing more about your customers is critical to the marketing effort. Every firm goes through distinct phases in its interaction with its customers: acquisition, retention and enhancement. It is important to define CRM goals for each phase. Clarifying current strategies and practices is vital before undertaking any CRM solution.

The business processes of the typical professional services firm interact with the customer at many different points.

- Acquisition data includes front-end developmental contacts of marketing, BD and sales
- Retention information includes data collected during the mid-cycle contracted services of design, engineering, construction, and post-construction service— this also includes the ongoing back office services of purchasing, billing and collections
- Enhancement data comes from the creation of customized services specific to each client's needs and preferences

When done correctly, the customer's experience can be documented and mined for trends, hiccups and successes. Consolidating, categorizing and analyzing that information and experience can provide invaluable data that would allow a company to

better serve each customer by providing services that anticipate their buying patterns, lower their budgets, exceed their expectations for quality and accelerate their typical scheduling requirements.

3.5.1 Select a CRM System

Some firms are without a company-wide CRM and are in need of one. Some have a centralized CRM, but no one within the firm wants to use it. Some actually use their CRM, but haven't been able to build a consensus on how to use it. Others have achieved an agreement on CRM usage across multiple offices, but have yet to institute systems to manage it.

Regardless of what stage a firm is facing, effective CRM can feel like an insurmountable task. Everyone has their own ideas and wants to head in their own direction. However, there are a few things that firms can do at the onset of implementation that can help them achieve enduring success.

First, clearly define the goals and objectives that your firm seeks to achieve. Here are some examples of statements of software needs you might come up with based on your objectives. CRM software must...

- Be centralized; a cloud-based or network-based CRM is acceptable
- Be intuitive and user-friendly; cumbersome databases will not make the short list
- Integrate with existing company hardware and software programs
- Be capable of auto-generating résumés and project profiles
- Have a mobile application for access by remote workers

TARGET POINT

Whatever your firm's objectives are, they should be clearly defined prior to conducting any CRM evaluation. In doing so, a firm is far better prepared to assess the overall benefits or the projected ROI of any system under consideration.

Once a firm has clearly defined its objectives, it should consider creating a broad evaluation team. There seems to be a prevailing tendency within the A/E/C industry to appoint only one or two individuals to evaluate short-listed CRM systems. These individuals are typically limited to IT professionals and firm executives. While their insights are extremely critical during this process, a solid CRM evaluation team should also include a variety of end-user representatives. Involving spokespeople from key groups like marketing, BD, project management and administration will ultimately provide a more holistic view of how the new system will be used within the firm. Involving a broad evaluation team can also increase the chances of end-user buy-in across multiple user groups once CRM implementation has commenced.

In selecting software suppliers and their solutions, it is important to check several factors. These include:

- **Stability.** The financial history/health of the company.
- **Customer service.** The ability to support an implementation.
- **Functionality.** Does it meet specific needs?
- **Flexibility.** Can it be customized?
- **Implementation.** Is it easy or difficult?
- **Price.** Is the value to cost ratio consistent with your goals?
- **Support.** Do they provide technical and training support during and after the implementation?

3.5.2   Outline the Data to Be Housed in the CRM

Using CRM technology to "mine" the database of characteristics (e.g., industry, size, location, etc.) of your existing client base can help identify the demographics of potential new customers. By cataloging a firm's project history and comparing the client demographics in the successful projects (i.e., projects that were profitable), you can identify the types of clients your firm should (or should not) pursue.

 TARGET POINT

Information is the key element that gives any firm a leg up on the competition. Whether private sector or public sector, the more information you can glean will help you create an appropriate and effective pursuit strategy for each opportunity.

Learning as much about a prospective client as possible can make the difference. Insights into the client's perspective of their real needs for a project often differentiate the winning firm from the rest of the shortlist. In profiling both existing and potential new clients, some questions to ask might include:

- What are their principal lines of business?
- How big are they?
- Where are they located geographically?
- Who are their competitors? (In the public sector, these could be other agencies competing for appropriations.)
- What is their history of building?
- Do they own or lease their properties?
- What is their history of capital expenditure for buildings (or infrastructure)?
- Does their current market growth support the need for more building?
- Do they have internal resources for designing, engineering or managing projects?

The advantage of a thorough profile is the potential for useful data reduction. The key is the development of an information base that includes the mass of potential

clients that can be filtered down to specific target groups. That data set can be further refined to specific postal codes to help define regional and local marketing efforts. With sufficient input data, the dimension of information can be focused down to the smallest imaginable level—the individual who can be traced by name and address.

CRM technology provides the means to move from generalization to the specific and identifiable. Another aspect of the profile is the type of information used. Generally it is research data combined with larger demographic trends. It can include changes in economic conditions or societal and behavioral attitudes. Which industries are growing? What business-types are expanding or consolidating? As the technology becomes more sophisticated, more tools are gained that can assist in forecasting future opportunities.

From a practical standpoint, gathering data should include as much consistency as possible. A single record (the information about a person, company or project) is only as good as the individual fields of specific data about that record (e.g., first name, last name, title, address, phone, etc.). Because so much of professional service marketing is person-to-person, it becomes imperative to ensure the completeness of all fields of the database. This applies equally to CRM at a small level (i.e., personal information or contact management software) as it does to large-scale implementations (i.e., enterprise-wide relational database that includes information on project history, costs and schedule).

Matching a service provider's strengths and offerings with client database demographics and a prospect list's characteristics yields the best matches and can establish the priority for the firm's marketing efforts. From this beginning point, it is easy to create customized communication pieces that are tailored to the immediate and long-term requirements of each qualified prospect. This information can then be used by the front line BD personnel to make sales calls that are more effective and more memorable.

DATA

Prioritizing the marketing effort with CRM technology helps avoid the "shotgun" approach, which blankets every possible customer with generic information. Accurate and useful data can help prioritize the firm's "reactive" response to the qualifications or proposal request that was not anticipated. It can also focus the firm on "proactive" marketing and selling to the customers most likely to buy your firm's services.

Once a CRM database of existing and potential customers is created, the profile information can be used to identify and qualify potential prospects. One of the great advantages of technology-based marketing is the ability to personalize the offer to the target market. The marketing effort is much more effective when comparative analysis is utilized. By closely matching the services offered to the needs of the potential clients with similar demographics to other, existing clients, the firms marketing effectiveness can be improved. Management guru, Tom Peters, established in his writing that selling the same services to existing clients is the easiest, followed by same services to like clients, followed by new services to existing clients. Following his advice will allow you to maintain your business in bad times, and grow your business when demand increases.

Reaching your target audience in the A/E/C industry requires a plan to determine the best sequence of contacts to communicate your message and the best sequence of increasingly tactical information to communicate to them. An effective CRM implementation helps produce and deliver appropriate collateral information that is specific to project requirements. It enables direct presentation of qualifications and solutions that focus on the new business prospect. While introducing your firm to the client can come as a result of relationships with other service providers in the industry, it is more effective when your database is setting the strategic direction to the potential clients you want as customers.

3.5.3 Implement the CRM System

The ever-popular strengths, weaknesses, opportunities and threats (SWOT) analysis helps businesses to create a clear picture of their market position, which then helps them to establish goals to maximize their strengths and mitigate their weaknesses. During this analysis, you get to know more about the companies or clients you work for—or want to work for—and you assess your competition as well.

After all of those hours spent researching your markets, clients and/or competition, how often do you refer back to that giant SWOT in the heat of a pursuit or when making key marketing decisions? How many of your firm's professionals refer back to the SWOT when going to visit a target client or preparing a proposal? It's clear this is valuable information, yet often these documents are left to gather dust.

There are some simple things you can add to your marketing information or CRM systems to keep your SWOT data easily accessible for decision making. If your firm isn't using a fully customizable CRM system—like Deltek Vision, Cosential, Salesforce, MS Dynamics, or even a home-grown system—you can adapt what follows by adding the documents to your structured file folders. Parcel out the pieces of your SWOT that are specific to target markets or clients and store them with related documents.

For those of you with more robust systems, consider creating customized fields that will allow you to track and store information on your prospective or current company/client profiles, such as:

- SWOT analyses specific to the company/client
- General statistics, history and news employees should know about each company/client, including vision or values statements, organizational charts or a list of major stakeholders, links to websites or capital improvement plans, links to past proposals or RFPs and any other information you would use or want access to regularly
- Information on disadvantaged/small business certifications (e.g., WBE, MBE, DBE, WSOB, etc.)
- Rate tables submitted in previous proposals or work

Depending on the depth of your firm's analyses, you can extend this to competitor profiles, target markets, project pursuits, events and other activities. By attaching this information in a visible location to your company/client profiles, you will make it easily accessible to all staff members who regularly play a role in contacting or communicating with clients. Plus, you can easily access and update the data so it no longer sits stagnant.

How your firm does business will determine the kind of information you'll want to track. A large firm with multiple national or multi-national offices will need a much more robust system than a small boutique design firm. Both will benefit from applying technology appropriately. Final decisions should be made based on goals and resources, and the determination of the extent to which technology will be incorporated into the operations of the business.

Typically, allow as much or more time as went into the CRM planning for the implementation of the technology. Keep in mind that any CRM system will need to grow with the business. Software should be upgradeable, allowing for growth and customizable to meet the specific needs and vocabulary common to the practice. Including network capabilities and multi-user licenses will allow for increasing the number of people who can utilize a technology-based system as the business grows.

Whether a simple personal information manager or a more robust sales automation toolset, the selection of the CRM engine should meet the demands of the company now and be able to expand into the future.

3.5.4   Maintain the CRM System

Develop a regular schedule for researching the clients and contacts in your CRM system to make sure that their information is still up-to-date. Focus on any contacts who have left their firm or whose emails have suddenly become incorrect (i.e., any emails you send them get returned to you). Look online—Google, LinkedIn and other social media sites are good ways of finding out the current location of your contact. If you cannot find them, mark them as "inactive" in your CRM so that no more communications go to the wrong address (either mail or email).

Follow up frequently on these contacts. If, after six months of research, you still cannot find current information for them, mark them as "dormant." After another six months of no luck, delete them from the database. As with the other knowledge management systems, assign one staff member the responsibility of updating the database and establish a schedule for doing so.

Create data entry protocols that dictate the style and content of the data entered into the system, such as how abbreviations should be written and the correct format for titles. These rules establish consistency within the CRM system as well as with the rest of the firm's systems.

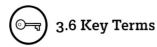 **3.6 Key Terms**

Below are the main terms covered in this section:

- Knowledge management
- Management information system (MIS)
- Decision support system (DSS)
- Lead tracking system
- Chief Information Officer (CIO)
- User group
- Customer relationship management (CRM)
- Strengths, Weaknesses, Opportunities, and Threats (SWOT) Analysis

4   Conduct Marketing Training Sessions

Training your marketing professionals to step up to a BD role can make a real difference to your company's bottom line. While not everyone is suitable to play a leading role in BD, you can identify and foster those employees who have that potential.

By the end of this section, you should understand the following key points, and be able to use them in the management of your marketing group:

- How to monitor and evaluate employee performance in light of the required BD skill set
- How to identify skill deficits, identify training resources and create a development plan for employees with the potential to play a BD role in the organization

4.1   Establish Outcome/Competency Alignment for Marketing, Business Development (BD) and Sales Positions

The entire firm should know and understand the marketing and BD plans and how each individual fits into the big picture. Everyone must become an active contributor to the marketing effort of a firm. You may need to explain in some detail the effort expected from each employee. You must observe people in their marketing and BD efforts and adjust the assignments as necessary. Review the roles for marketing and BD staff that were described in section 1. Make sure that the employees who hold those roles right now are the right people for the job.

It's difficult to force non-BD professionals to want to do BD. One way of thinking about the difference between marketing and BD is that marketing is everything that's done behind the scenes (e.g., updating the website and social media, developing marketing collateral, establishing the firm's brand, etc.), while BD takes the tools created by the marketing staff and uses them out in the world to bring in work. By drawing the distinction between the two roles in this way, you can see why someone who is not comfortable attending crowded events or public speaking would shy away from BD activities. It's just not their role!

While skills like networking, public speaking and proposal writing are likely to prove valuable to any professional, it seems that each specialist may be better served by capitalizing on their strengths and unique skill set rather than working to overcome their weaknesses with skills that they may not ever feel comfortable demonstrating in a professional environment. For instance, if a draftsman is skilled in his craft and highly valuable to his firm on account of the complex drawings he produces, his value to the firm diminishes when he spends time away from his desk developing skills that are irrelevant to his work. On the contrary, time spent in a professional development environment that expands upon his natural abilities serves to enhance his value to the firm while allowing others with similar natural abilities (in marketing, for instance) to grow and thrive within their comfort zone. When one works in collaboration with the other, the firm benefits from the natural skill sets inherent in each.

Yet the best firms address cross-functional training in two directions—operations staff, say, learns marketing skills and marketing staff learns operations skills. This way, the staff of each functional area is well-versed on the needs and opportunities presented by their teammates in the other department. The goal in going through this process is for each department to gain a better understanding of how best to work together toward client satisfaction.

4.2   Conduct a Training Needs Assessment

From the moment a new hire hits the door, their experience of the new culture is being formed. Everything you can do to make that individual successful in your organization helps the marketing team. Introducing the technical personnel to the world of sales and the role they could play is important to build the team. Educating the entire firm on your various markets, projects and wins also bolsters the army of recruits.

From writing seminars to presentation training, everyone who markets for your firm can benefit from increasing their skills. Marketing professionals should be trained consistently on the structure of the company, their role and specific technical skills that will help them contribute meaningfully to the success of your firm.

Conduct a training needs analysis as soon as you hire a new employee so that you can identify the areas they are weak in and provide opportunities for them to improve the skills that will make them better in their roles. Ways to determine an employee's training needs include the following tools:

- **Observation.** What do their first deliverables look like? How comfortable do they seem in performing (or learning to perform) the various tasks they'll be responsible for?

- **Individual interviews.** Once an employee has settled in a bit, ask them about their skill set directly. What do they see as their weaknesses? What areas would they like to learn more about?

- **Group questionnaires.** This is a good way to determine what skills need to be bolstered across an entire team or department.

Of course, don't only conduct a needs analysis with new hires—all of your employees could benefit from the development of a systematic process for identifying and addressing their needs.

The assessment tool provided in SMPS Blueprints (referenced previously in section 1) can be used to help the professional services marketer or business developer define where they are on their career path and what skills they need to master in order to advance their career. The analysis could help your staff conduct a personal inventory of their knowledge and skills in their current position, and identify areas where they are strong or need improvement. Use this assessment—or something like it—to highlight "gaps" between your staff's current knowledge and what they need to know in order to best perform their roles.

It may also be advantageous to use personality assessments to help teams grasp their own behavior patterns and tendencies. Personality tests like DiSC®, Color Code

Personality Profile, and Myers Briggs can help a team take a fresh look at itself and recognize strategies to influence new and different types of people. You may also want to do activity-oriented surveys to understand who's doing what and who's avoiding what related to marketing or BD. Initial, midpoint and post-benchmarking surveys provide fast-track metrics to measure your success. These tools are important because they help individuals understand themselves better. They also help leaders understand the team better and trainers calibrate their programs more directly to the participants.

4.3   Identify Training Resources

Once you've conducted a staff assessment, review the results and identify subject areas where many in your team could use more training. One of the benefits of a group questionnaire, or other firm-wide assessment tool, is that you can use it to match up employees who are lacking in one knowledge area or skill set to other staff members who are particularly experienced in that subject.

Employees who are experts in an area can be asked to give a presentation to the rest of the firm during lunch, or at a formal training session. For subjects that no internal staff have experience with, look to external resources. Identify a list of speakers who could be hired to come in and share their knowledge.

> **TARGET POINT**
>
> A word about the importance of finding a good speaker: Highly interactive training requires high energy; when the instructor is energized, he or she engages the audience and the audience becomes energized, too. The instructors must be knowledgeable about their subject. Most importantly, they must be passionate.

4.4   Develop a Schedule/Calendar of Training Programs

Brainstorm a list of potential training programs based on your needs assessment. Some of these needs will be good candidates for addressing at a more informal, recurring program, such as a "lunch and learn." Lunch and learns are typically one hour long and occur during regular business hours, where lunch is provided for the staff. Find a recurring date (e.g., monthly, bi-monthly, quarterly, etc.) where minimal conflicts exist and add these trainings to the corporate calendar.

Other needs might require a longer, more focused approach to training. For example, as a benefit and enhancement for its technical staff, George Butler Associates established an innovative training program called "Marketing University." The idea, first conceived during an annual retreat of the firm's marketing department, was a high-quality, multi-dimensional program consisting of specific programs on such topics as networking, cold calling, presentations, ethics, and tradeshows, among others.

When planning training, consider the size of the audience and the budget available for training before determining the type of training. For BD training, for example, the audience should include all individuals who are responsible for winning work for the firm, including the proposal staff.

The most effective training is hands-on. By providing multi-sensory methods of teaching (e.g., verbal, documentation and practice) you will yield the greatest retention. Ask questions and put the answers on a flip chart. Provide mock interviews. Allow users to access laptops to enter client data into the corporate BD database throughout the process. Ask participants to write paragraphs for proposals, or to even make a presentation to a fictitious client. And during each exercise, gather feedback.

People learn best when they are engaged and outside of their comfort zone. They are more attuned when observing others and receiving feedback. Some people may feel very uncomfortable with the exercises. Others may excel. The idea is to generate a risk-free learning environment, where participants are taught a process, skill or tool and then allowed to practice, get feedback and practice again. Provide feedback to the participants' supervisors on what the participants know and do well and recommend areas for improvement. These elements can be incorporated into short-term and long-term performance goals.

And remember: training should be a little fun. BD training, for example, should simulate the "real world"—it should employ some competitiveness. Perhaps the participants are divided into teams that compete for a fictitious pursuit with a fictitious client. Highlighting the winning teams at an annual meeting or in company-wide emails, gives credence to the training program and imparts a sense of a BD culture. Most importantly, sharing the message with everyone in the firm helps to build the BD culture.

During the design of the training program, the person responsible for its design and development should solicit a diverse (e.g., gender, ethnic, geographic and service) team to provide feedback on the training materials and to serve as instructors or in supporting roles as activity facilitators (e.g., the fictitious client).

One underlying objective of training is networking, especially in mid-sized to larger firms. Take advantage of getting a team of individuals together who may not typically work together. Use examples of real pursuits and real clients not just for the training, but to share with them other types of projects you have and where they are located, especially in larger firms. This has the added benefit of helping your staff gain the information needed to cross-sell your firm's services, as discussed in section 2.

4.5   Evaluate and Refine Programs

If there's one misconception in skill-building, it's that once you learn it, you've got it. Wrong. Professional development is plagued by people knowing too much and deploying too little. They know what to do, but it's not showing up in the workplace. That requires a maintenance plan, which should have three parts to it. First, tie each training event to individual private coaching clinics so people can talk through and troubleshoot their own specific issues. Second, put into place a regulation plan, such as monthly "ambassador meetings" where you talk about the ambassador role, identify and resolve questions, and acknowledge and reward success.

Third, bring these steps into discussions around high-stakes communications like interviews, negotiations and important meetings. Under pressure, most people fall back to their defaults, and forget to follow the process they trained for. By reinforcing learning points, and using them in high-, medium-, and low-pressure communication, they can be taught, practiced and reinforced to show up in your workplace.

Don't ever give up on a training program too soon. Instead of trashing a program that doesn't seem to be working, try first to figure out why. Is the venue too far away? Are the speakers all stiff and boring? Maybe your staff knows more about the content than you'd thought, and they don't feel like they're learning anything. Provide evaluation forms at the end of each event to gauge feedback and the relevance of the material. Ask your staff for ideas on subjects they would like to learn more about, and adjust the calendar of events as necessary.

 4.6   **Key Terms**

Below are the main terms covered in this section:

- Cross-functional training
- Lunch and learn

5   Attend Professional Development Activities

Participating in professional organizations can be a path to personal development as well as a means to generate new business. You can learn to identify which associations will result in the greatest ROI, and you can help your employees turn participation into important networking opportunities.

By the end of this section, you should understand the following key points, and be able to use them in the management of your marketing group:

- How to help your staff members identify suitable professional organizations and encourage their participation
- The importance of teaching your employees to develop and maintain a professional network

5.1   Identify Expectations for Staff Involvement

People join organizations and associations in order to advance their personal and professional goals. Review your staff members' Professional Development Plans to help them identify their areas of interest, and discuss their current position within the firm and how that position aligns with their interests. The next step is to determine which organizations you and your staff should target for participation.

There are literally tens of thousands of professional organizations, representing virtually every profession. The A/E/C industry is well-represented, with organizations supporting the needs of marketers, architects, engineers, designers, contractors, subcontractors and owners. Moreover, there are Chambers of Commerce, rotaries and other business clubs that have been formed for people and firms in a specific geographic area and are thus not focused on a specific industry or profession. There are also educational, scientific and charitable membership organizations that may often interact with some of these other organizations.

In some organizations, you can join as an individual; in others, your firm is the basic structure for membership. The type of firm for which you work, and your role within that firm, will direct you to the most useful professional organizations for you and your firm. For example, if you work primarily as a marketer within the A/E/C industry, then you probably already belong to SMPS. If you are in sales and/or marketing for a construction management or design-build firm, then you may also need to belong to the Construction Management Association of America (CMAA) or the Design-Build Institute of America (DBIA).

If you work with architects, then the American Institute of Architects (AIA) is a key organization for you. Befriend some members of the Society of Industrial and Office Realtors (SIOR), and you'll also learn about proposed projects that may become marketing opportunities for you. If you sell or market for an engineering firm that relies on business from other engineers, then you may want to have your company become part of the American Council of Engineering Companies (ACEC). If your firm has a healthcare specialty, then the American Society for Healthcare Engineering (ASHE) will provide leads as well as expand your knowledge of healthcare facilities.

Membership in professional organizations need not be limited to an individual's profession or industry. There are other opportunities to consider. Think about joining an organization or two where your company's key clients are members. For example, let's say that hospitals are a major portion of your business. In this situation, ASHE is an option. Not only would you learn more about your clients' healthcare business and their concerns, but you could improve your relationships by this additional time spent together.

If your clients are on any committees, it might behoove you to get on them also. This is especially important if any of your competition is trying to get closer to your clients by also joining these organizations. The easiest way to find out about which professional organizations your clients belong to is to ask them. Other indirect ways are to look for certification or membership certificates in their office and publications on their desk or in their lobby.

Sometimes memberships in your clients' organizations are not open to those not active in their profession or industry. If this is the case, ask about the availability of associate membership. Some professional organizations offer these restricted memberships to individuals who are not directly involved in their industry.

5.2   Identify Organizations to Participate In

The first step in selecting the right professional organization(s) to join is to determine your priorities. If your primary job responsibility is marketing, priorities for organization membership might include the opportunity for professional growth, improved industry knowledge, increased lead generation, increased knowledge of clients' business and improved rapport with clients.

On the other hand, if you are a senior manager in a firm and marketing is only a secondary responsibility, your priorities might focus more on enhancing general management skills, strengthening client relationships and increasing your marketing skills.

Overall, your reasons for joining a professional organization should fall into one or more of the following categories:

- BD and networking
- Continuing education
- Charitable/community participation

The primary purposes of these organizations is to help their members conduct their business more professionally and to provide for the professional development of its members. Professional organizations develop educational programs, publish insightful books and studies and, in general, constantly strive to upgrade the understanding of members in a given profession or industry and help keep them on top of emerging technological and special developments. Conferences, both regional and national, and other types of meetings provide periodic opportunities to reaffirm shared values, establish and realign relationships, and conduct work, have fun and thereby build relationships with other people in the same profession or industry.

In addition, a fair number of professional organizations in the United States offer a certification program for individuals engaged in their profession or industry. Certification programs provide standards of excellence that all members of the organization can work toward. The certification program in SMPS is the CPSM–Certified Professional Services Marketer.

Members who gain certification benefit by increased professional competence, increased respect and recognition in the industry or profession, increased opportunity for upward mobility, credibility and increased self-esteem. Professional certification also demonstrates an individual's overall level of competency. This kind of credential is specifically designed to distinguish those who have proven knowledge and expertise from the masses who "claim" to be experts.

The following are additional benefits that can be gained through membership in an organization. Determine which benefits are most important to you, and judge potential organizations by their ability to provide you with the benefits you are looking for.

- **New business opportunities.** Membership in a professional organization breeds familiarity with the organization, familiarity builds relationships, these relationships build trust and trusting relationships facilitate referrals, which are valuable commodities for new business opportunities. There is also the special advantage of being seen at the organization's various programs and functions, particularly at the regional and national conferences where many more members are present. Members that are in the "top of the mind" of other members have a greater chance of being contacted during the year for referrals, joint ventures and new business opportunities. This sure beats cold calling!

- **Communications and joint research with member firms.** It is in the mutual interest of members and their firms to share information and research findings with similar industry firms. Organizations can develop and administer joint research efforts, whereby many firms shoulder the costs and share benefits of the research. This helps members and their firms work smarter, grow faster and avoid costly mistakes.

- **Networking and learning opportunities.** The existing membership network means it is easy for any member to get information, including business leads. Conversations with other members at, or between, the various sponsored programs provide new ideas, validate existing concepts and stimulate creativity.

- **Image enhancement.** Membership in a professional organization tells everyone that the member and his or her company are actively involved in that profession or industry and are making contributions to further its growth and status.

- **Face time with existing clients.** Attending an association's regularly scheduled functions is an efficient way to visit with many clients in a short time.

- **Advertising and marketing activities.** Many organizations develop and place media advertising for their members' services. Moreover, many organizations

offer their members a broad array of information and discussion services, including a publication or resource library, a newsletter, an online directory, a ListServ, online forums, job openings and blogs.

- **Government relations activities.** For virtually every organization and association, interaction with government entities is critical. The government-relations arm of the organization can serve as the construction industry's voice with the legislative, executive, and judicial branches of the federal government, as well as with state and local governments and news media. For the A/E/C industry, these activities may include:

  o Providing members with an structure to deal with issues on an industry-wide basis

  o Promoting the business interests of the members firms to Congress, federal agencies, state and local governments, and international organizations

  o Promoting and securing Fair Labor Standards Act rules to protect firms from unfair enforcement actions

  o Securing A/E/C tax deductions

  o Promoting the use of Qualifications-Based Selection (QBS) at all levels of public and private sector procurement

  o Fighting repeated attempts to shut down government outsourcing

After the priorities are determined, the next step is to locate the professional organization(s) that can help you the most. The best place to begin is to discuss your requirements with your business associates, peers, clients and friends. They should be able to point you in the right direction.

 IDEA

Review an organization's website or attend some meetings to learn more about them. Most professional organizations allow visitors to attend. Most also will allow your firm to join as an associate member if your firm doesn't qualify for regular membership.

When you've narrowed down your options to a short list of organizations you or your staff are interested in joining, do some digging. Find out information about the organization, including the following:

- Vision and mission statement
- Types of members (e.g., clients, consultants, competitors, vendors, etc.)
- Educational opportunities

- Frequency of meetings
- Composition of board members and committees
- Feasibility that someone from your firm will be able to join committees or get onto the board of directors

Knowing at least this much about an organization will help you to decide whether your staff is eligible to join, and also whether joining will give you the payoff you're looking for.

5.3   Train Staff to Network

When we think about networking, we usually think of it as a means of obtaining leads. Certainly, lead generation is one of the most important uses of networking; however, there is a great deal more to be gained by having and using a network. A network can also be used to get a personal introduction to a prospect. You can use it for market research. You can find out what other firms see as market trends and where the action will be. You can get information about the competition, their strengths and their weaknesses. And you can use a network to confirm or disqualify rumors. If Corporation X announces it is expanding, first check with the network to see if that expansion is real, if it's already been committed, or if it is a potential project for your firm. An effective network can save you a lot of time and your firm a lot of money because you won't be chasing jobs that aren't real or for which you are not qualified. And if the project is real, an effective network can give you valuable information that can help you win the job.

The major job of a marketer is to help the firm get work. Having an effective network enhances a marketer's ability to get work. Therefore, good networking adds to marketers' value to their firms. A well-constructed and effectively used network will significantly improve a marketer's contribution to his or her firm's efforts to get additional projects and obtain information that is uniquely valuable to the firm. Training your staff to network comfortably and effectively will exponentially increase your firm's reach of information.

So, how does one network? How does it work? For the core members of your network, it starts with establishing a one-on-one relationship with that person. This requires a face-to-face meeting where you establish that you each have a mutual interest in exchanging information about the industry. This is why membership with a professional organization is so useful. But it goes past the initial meeting—networking is a long-term process based on developing and cultivating relationships. This can be done through a breakfast, a lunch, or just setting aside 30 minutes over a cup of coffee.

Before you attend a function put on by your professional organization, make sure that you are prepared to make the most of this networking opportunity. Research the organization, and determine the membership composition. Identify members that you or your staff member would like to meet so you can be on the lookout for this person at the function. However, don't get carried away targeting people who you think can do something for you and your firm; networking is about helping others, not about trying

to get others to help you. Think of it as an exchange of information.

Tips for Networking at a Function

- Always have your business cards on hand. You never know when you'll meet someone you want to keep in touch with.

- Bring a friend to reduce anxiety (but don't rely on them to keep you company all night).

- Sit at a table where you don't know anyone. You'll never expand your circle if you're always looking for a familiar face.

- Look for people who are standing or sitting alone and go talk to them.

- Always listen more than you speak.

- Look for ways you can help people. This includes sharing useful information, making an introduction, and suggesting leads.

- Follow up! After the event, send an email or make a phone call to the people you've met.

5.3.1   Information Sharing

So, what information is valuable to others? What information should and should not be shared? Positive information about your firm is the easiest and sometimes the most valuable information you can share. That you have made a shortlist or, better yet, that you have been awarded a new project is fun information to share and is valuable for those further down the feeding chain that have an opportunity to provide other services or supply materials for the project.

Remember, just because you lost the job doesn't mean that you don't have valuable information. The others in your network that are still looking forward to participating on that project need to know who got it. You can make yourself equally valuable to your network by sharing with them who did get the job. It's not as much fun, but it still needs to be shared.

Information about the market is tradeable information. If you went to a meeting or convention and heard a valuable speech about a market or sector of the market, think about those in your network who were not there but could profit from that information. Send them the handout or write a one-page summary and share with members of that network.

To be a valuable member of a network, you must share information that is valuable to the other person. Increase your value by thinking about how the person on the receiving end can use the information you want to share. If they are not in the healthcare market, information you gained at that healthcare conference will probably be of little use to them. Increase your value by sharing the most valuable information with only those few people in your network who help you the most or to anchor a new networking relationship. Sharing valuable information too freely decreases your value in the network.

TARGET POINT

Some information, such as information told to you in confidence, is not to be shared. Information about specific fees is usually considered not tradeable. In addition, information that is internal to your firm should not be passed on. Keep your skeletons in the closet.

Keep in mind that the information you share with others has an impact on how they view you and your firm. You can use this to your advantage to enhance your position in the industry and to position your firm for future work. If your firm has a growing portfolio in a specific building type and wants to grow in that market niche, let your network know of your interest. They can alert you to opportunities in the market and they will talk up your expertise to others.

5.3.2   Keep in Touch

The primary rule of networking is staying in touch. You don't have to take time for a personal meeting, you don't have to play a better game of telephone tag. That handout from that speech will keep you in touch with a valuable part of the network. Just don't forget to put your name on it, so they will know who sent it. Stapling a business card to what you are sending is the simplest way.

Some information is for everyone in your network, like the information you learned from an article in Real Estate Forum that others might have missed. Some information is for a chosen one or two—those people with whom you have been exchanging specific information about a specific lead because you are both in a unique position to gain information. Don't be too free with your most valuable information. If you are careful about with whom you share what, you will be a more valued member of your network.

Choose a core group of people to develop a long-term relationship with, and keep them at the forefront of your mind whenever you learn something new. Send articles that you think they would be interested in (for example, those concerning an issue you talked about the last time you had lunch), invite them to industry events—basically, let them know that you are looking out for them. If they feel that you genuinely want to help them succeed, they will want to find opportunities to help you, too.

TARGET POINT
Friends, Not Rivals

Rita, an architect, was at her son's gymnastics meet when she met another parent, Bob (also an architect), in the stands. While they were chatting, he mentioned a project that his architecture firm was just starting work on. Rita said it sounded similar to one she had recently finished. She shared with Bob some of the lessons she learned from her experience and gave him some tips. She wasn't consciously networking while they talked, just glad to have a new friend to talk to while waiting for her son's routine to start. But Bob was so excited to meet someone who was more interested in helping him than in promoting her own firm that he invited her to come and talk with his principal-in-charge of the project about her suggestions. They exchanged contact information before the end of the meet.

The next week, Rita visited Bob's firm and discussed with the principal-in-charge how they could meet their project's objectives and avoid the obstacles she had run into during her own project. She wasn't making a sales pitch—she didn't even leave a pamphlet behind when she left. Still, the principal considered her ideas so good and her willingness to help so genuine that he called her up the next day and asked for a proposal to join their team as a consultant.

Key Concepts for this Story:
- You never know when the opportunity to network may present itself
- Networking doesn't have to be intimidating; it can be as easy as making a new friend
- Just being genuinely helpful can be a great way to showcase your own abilities

5.4   Develop Your Professional Network

Educate your staff on the benefits of developing and enlarging their professional networks throughout their careers. Developing professional relationships with others in their industry will lead to long-term personal growth and development: friendships will bloom, information sharing will come more frequently and easily, and new business opportunities will arise.

However, it's not enough to merely be a member and show up now and again at functions—long-term success in an organization is directly related to the effort you put in. In other words: you reap what you sow. To really get the most out of any membership in a professional organization, you have to become actively involved in that organization. Besides learning more about your profession or industry, members who take on a leadership role also improve their skills in leadership, in management, and in public speaking; and they learn how to work better with clients, the media and large groups of people.

Members who are on committees or who serve as officers of the organization also achieve a certain added distinction and credibility, not to mention visibility. In addition, members who take on a leadership role have a greater voice in how the organization will continue to contribute to their own professional development. Should the time ever come when you find yourself in the position of having to find a new job, prospective new employers will look very favorably on the leadership roles you had while a member of professional organizations.

5.5   Assess the ROI of Participation

Before a member of your staff renews their annual membership to an organization, have a discussion about what they've gained from their participation over the past year. How many events did they attend? How many new contacts have they gained as a direct result of attending? What have they learned through their participation? Compare the costs of membership and active participation (e.g., travel expenses, time spent at events that could have been spent on other work, etc.) to the benefits gained.

Also discuss the potential that your staff member has for getting more involved in the organization, and therefore gaining more from their membership. Is there the opportunity for committee participation? Could they land a seat on the board of directors? What are the possibilities of firm sponsorship? Becoming a sponsor of the professional organization could gain your firm additional recognition and exposure to the members within the organization. Sometimes becoming a sponsor comes with additional privileges, such as complimentary or discounted lunches or attendance at events; verbal, print and online recognition by an organization; and even a privileged seat on the organization's committee or board.

Determine together whether continuing participation in the organization will be worth their effort.

 ## 5.6 Key Terms

Below are the main terms covered in this section:

- Networking
- Information sharing
- Sponsorship

6   Recruit Personnel

Attracting the right people to work with you is key to your success, both personally and as an organization. You must not only reach out in innovative ways, but you must also present your firm as an attractive place to work. Fortunately, today's technology affords many creative ways to reach out to potential recruits.

By the end of this section, you should understand the following key points, and be able to use them in the management of your marketing group:

- How to work with HR to clarify the positions you are trying to fill and craft job descriptions that are focused and likely to generate interest
- The considerations involved in creating a website that represents your firm's culture
- How to get your hiring message out in as many appropriate venues as possible

6.1   Coordinate with HR

Talent is a key building block for a successful practice. Beyond securing the right clients, you also need to help your firm attract and retain the professionals who can effectively deliver the expertise that you are selling.

The responsibility for developing and retaining talent within A/E/C firms is typically shared by practice leaders and HR management. Practice leaders are tasked with creating knowledge and intellectual capital, as well as staffing and utilization. HR is responsible for the framework of employment—policies, procedures, guidelines, compensation and benefits—as well as talent development and training. Working together, they collaborate on recruiting (in most firms HR leads the recruiting process) and the practice's leadership oversees qualification and selection.

Today, as marketing responsibilities continue to broaden and become more complex, it's time for A/E/C marketers to take more of a leadership role in shaping the future of your firms by actively engaging in the pursuit of talent. Marketers should be proactive about reaching out to HR staff. See if HR will give you a copy of what they're handing out at a career fair so you can assist in improving the graphics or copy or offer to help edit and review an employment ad before it goes out to the local newspaper.

TARGET POINT

Recruitment may be more of an HR job, but marketers will have more experience writing and designing announcements, creating content for various mediums (e.g., website, LinkedIn, YouTube, TV, print, radio, social media, etc.), and other tasks related to selling a service. Offer your expertise to HR staff to ensure the best results.

6.2   Write Job Descriptions

A/E/C firms are social businesses, not in the traditional sense of being established to address a social problem, but in the newer model—organizations that are deeply integrating social media and social methodologies throughout the company to drive real business impact. A/E/C marketers are naturally focused on connecting with their internal and external audiences. They understand how the various parts of their firm work together to create a more powerful, integrated organization. They know how to collaborate with practice and management leaders to enhance their firm's overall platform of practice. They excel at articulating their firm's distinctive identity. They consistently promote their firm and communicate its culture. They continually develop content and use existing and emerging platforms to reach specific audiences.

And they are increasingly taking advantage of inbound marketing, a term originally coined by Brian Halligan of HubSpot to describe efforts that ultimately serve to bring customers closer to the brand. These activities complement—and, in some cases, outperform—the traditional outbound marketing activities of generating leads through cold calling, trade shows or advertising.

So, how can you leverage your skills, expertise and potential to attract and nurture the best people to work in and lead your firm?

To answer that question, you must first answer another: What drives your clients? It's not always a rush towards better, faster and cheaper. A/E/C marketers understand that they are able to craft value propositions to resonate with clients in specific markets and locations. In the talent business, it's important to understand the components of your value propositions as well—the things your firm can offer that set it apart from the rest.

Traditionally, the key motivation factors that drive people (especially knowledge workers) are:

- Interest in the work itself
- Opportunity for growth
- A sense of accomplishment
- Earned recognition

In Drive, Daniel H. Pink further explains that most people are energized by three fundamental things: autonomy (the freedom to direct our lives), mastery (our craving to excel), and purpose (the yearning for our work to serve something larger than ourselves).

How can working at your firm fulfill these needs for job seekers? This is the question you need to answer in your recruitment announcements. Use your marketing team's writing and graphic design skills (or turn to support staff) to work with HR in developing recruitment announcements that capture your audience's attention. In addition, make sure that your announcements are consistent with company standards and that they accurately convey your firm's culture.

 TARGET POINT

Consider your target audience for each job posting. Which generation do you expect to fill the position? A higher-level position that requires decades of experience is more likely to go to a Baby Boomer than a Millennial, and the announcement's design and copy should be crafted with this audience in mind.

6.3 Highlight Your People

Until recently, visitors to most A/E/C firm websites might come to the conclusion that the stunning buildings they viewed had designed and built themselves. That's because the static, sterile project images that populated most home pages served as artistic objects to admire rather than as inhabitable spaces created by people and for people. Deliberately missing was any sense of a human presence.

Gradually, this online portfolio approach to positioning a firm has given way to a more people-inclusive attitude. In most cases, the beautiful project images continue to lead the conversation, but they are no longer disconnected from the teams and individuals who bring these environments to life. People are continuing to escape from the back corners of a careers page and take up residence throughout all sections of a site.

"Clients hire people, not firms," says John Gilmore, vice president and senior writer at HOK. "Featuring people is important on a website, because in the end it's the people—not the firm—that they will be working with."

This enlightened perspective also reflects the recognition that potential employees are increasingly interested in learning about the work environment and culture of a potential employer before they will even consider coming onboard. But convincing a firm's leadership to embrace the idea of showcasing people requires busting the traditional HR concern that doing so would make the firm vulnerable to recruiters and competitors eager to hire them away.

Implementing a people-rich web strategy may require devoting a larger percentage of the marketing budget to commissioning professional people photos. Having an extensive library of engaging people shots—especially candid pictures of teams interacting and having fun together—is particularly helpful for showcasing a firm's culture and thought leadership within broader online news and social communities.

This approach also acknowledges the reality that potential employees—and clients—have numerous opportunities to learn about a firm outside the confines of its formal website. That's why the new generation of web platforms supports and enables the many possible ways in which individuals may visit, interact with and click from a website to other online communities.

TARGET POINT
Taking People to New Places: SmithGroupJJR

Rather than tucking its employees neatly into the "People" section of its new website, SmithGroupJJR has brought them front and center.

"One of our goals was to showcase the culture and personality of the firm," says Susan Arneson, SmithGroupJJR vice president and corporate marketing director. "We put a lot of effort into creating a site for sharing our culture, not only with clients but also with potential employees."

The site actively highlights the expertise, personalities, and interests of its employees, both within and beyond the workplace. Not only can you search for individuals by role and expertise, but you can also sort for those who identify themselves as a "Bookworm," "Foodie," "Sports Nut," or "World Traveler." When you mouse over a person's professional headshot, it reveals their non-work mode—perhaps kayaking on a lake, shooting hoops, or pushing a child on a swing.

Key Concepts for this Story:
- Use your current employees' stories to sell potential recruits on the benefits of working at your firm
- Put your firm's culture front and center in your recruitment efforts to be sure you attract like-minded employees

6.4   Promote the Job Opening

Develop separate announcements/campaigns for all media types—print, video, social media, etc.—but make sure that the message and information you're sending out through each campaign is consistent with the rest. And no matter where potential candidates find out about the job opening, direct them back to your website for more information on how to apply. Marketing your website in this way will provide job seekers with a repository of information about why they should work at your firm. The projects you work on, the people you work with, and how much fun employees have working for your firm are all displayed on your website (or should be!), so the best way to make sure that job seekers are exposed to that information is by running all applications through that site.

Don't forget to use your social and professional networks as well! Distribute final recruitment announcements to all of your employees and ask them to share it with their families, friends and colleagues. Post the announcement on LinkedIn, Facebook, Twitter, personal blogs and other social media networks. Send the announcement to all of the professional organizations with whom your firm is involved. Get the message out there through any means you can think of—you never know where your firm's next star employee will come from.

 TARGET POINT
Crossing Continents: T.Y. Lin International

LinkedIn is helping T.Y. Lin International reach outside the walls of its website to target potential employees in both the United States and Asia.

The global engineering firm is running two separate ad campaigns on the social networking platform. In the first five months since launching a "Follow Us" campaign, T.Y. Lin has attracted a 40 percent increase of followers to its branded company page. A separate "Work with Us" display ad, which appears on specific employee profiles, contributed to a 90 percent increase in unique visitors checking out specific job opportunities on the company's career page in the first month.

"We shifted some of our ad impressions to Asia a couple of months ago, and we've noticed a difference in visitors coming from Asia," says Maribel Castillo, associate vice president and director of corporate communications. "It's a good way to further establish a connection between our domestic and international operations."

Key Concepts for this Story:
- Networking sites such as LinkedIn have become an important means of targeting potential employees
- The key to a successful online recruitment campaign is continually updating content in a way that will be meaningful to job seekers

6.4.1   Assess Your Results

Once you've finished the recruitment process for a job opening, take a look at how it went. How did most people hear about the position? Where was your reach the largest? Generate individualized web links to determine the ROI from various announcements. Google Analytics can offer you a wealth of information about how people are finding certain pages on your website, how long they are spending there, where else they visit after checking out the job opening page and much more. Make sure that you are tracking this data for later analysis.

Measure and quantify the results for each media type and review the results with HR to determine whether each media outlet should be used again for future announcement postings.

6.5   Market Your Firm as the Most Attractive Choice

Here are some ways that marketing and HR can work together to elevate your firm's inbound recruiting efforts:

- **Create a great tagline.** Google's career website encourages visitors to "Do cool things that matter." Not surprisingly, it's cool graphically, too.

- **Have fun with video.** The Dallas office of Perkins + Will filmed Fitness Friday 2014. It's posted on YouTube and is also featured on the firm's Ideas+Buildings blog. According to chief talent officer Meg Brown, the video has generated a lot of interest from job applicants. Another good YouTube video is "CBT Delivers."

- **Write great ad copy.** Yes, there are important legal issues to consider in recruiting and hiring, but there's no reason why job postings need to be boring. The MulvannyG2 career site—Want to Work Here?—draws visitors in with, "Imagine the job of a lifetime. Now, open your eyes—it's all right here...."

- **Promote your talent message.** Seek new places to include your talent tagline—the back of business cards, email signature lines, social media accounts, white papers, YouTube and more.

- **Reinforce motivational themes.** Find opportunities to strengthen the messages that resonate with employees and potential employees—opportunity, accomplishment, recognition, purpose, social responsibility and sustainable design.

- **Create targeted publications.** Known for excellence in marketing communications, Gensler has done it again with Gensler's Student + Graduate Career Guide—a PDF available for download on the firm's Careers web page.

- **Rethink your website.** First, have up-to-date information and images. Second, go mobile. Third, make talent a priority. Kudos to Jacobs Engineering Group. Not only do they have "Join Us" as the first tab in the main navigation menu, but "Apply for a job" is in the footer. Throughout the website, their photos emphasize diversity, including many featuring women professionals.

- **Start a conversation.** It's not enough to collect applications in a database. Just as firms need effective marketers, they also need talent spotters who will open the door to building relationships with people who might become your next generation of leaders.

6.6   Look to Other Sources of Talent

Which generations are you targeting with your marketing and communications programs? For years, A/E/C clients have been primarily Baby Boomers and Gen X. As the new technology businesses emerged, Gen Y (Millennials) clients have started to appear. Today, Baby Boomers are retiring, and Gen X is less than 20 percent of the total adult population. The tech-savvy Millennials are not only your newest employees, but they are actively moving into leadership positions in your firms and in client firms. Spend time learning about the Millennial Generation to gain a better understanding of how to interact with and appeal to this important demographic group.

Millennials are mobile. Anything less is out of date and has serious potential to turn them off. A recent survey conducted by Glassdoor.com found that 89 percent of job seekers say their mobile device is an important tool for their job search. Twenty-five

percent would not apply to a job if a company's career site is not mobile-optimized. Ten percent use the mobile device during an interview to show off technical skills and past achievements.

Millennials are not only digital natives, they are also peer-oriented and globally concerned. They trust the opinions of people they know. They tend to be inclusive and welcome diversity, they have been actively involved in community service and seek others who support social responsibility and they are green. They are the ones who got the other generations to be mindful about the environment, cutting up those plastic six-pack holders and reducing waste. They aren't going to expect anything less from their employers.

These are themes that you can use to strategic advantage in your efforts to attract, engage and connect with internal and external audiences in a way that will develop and reinforce the pipeline of relationships that you need in order to build business and market for talent.

Setting up a booth at college career fairs is a good way to identify new talent—students who will soon be entering the workforce for internships or entry-level positions. While much of your trade show expertise can be applied to this environment, recognize the difference in your target market and adjust your approach accordingly. Select staff to work the exhibit who can answer questions about work life, career opportunities, and company culture, and who will relate well to Millennials. Sell the culture of your firm and career opportunities in your display and literature. Give away items that will appeal to this market—don't recycle your conference giveaways. And, of course, follow up with interested candidates and make swift hiring decisions. Great candidates are snatched up quickly.

 6.7 Key Terms

Below are the main terms covered in this section:

- Human Resources (HR)
- Inbound marketing
- Millennials
- Baby Boomers
- Gen X

7   Comply With Business and Accounting Principles

Keeping track of the bottom line is largely a matter of understanding basic accounting principles. You don't need an accounting degree to understand how sales and collections or staff overhead affects profitability. You can also get a handle on basic contract principles and what your contractual obligations are at different stages of the project lifecycle.

By the end of this section, you should understand the following key points and be able to use them to help better understand key metrics that help drive the success of a design firm:

- How to understand the basic accounting principles that are key to understanding a firm's financial statement

- The project lifecycle provides a map of what to expect at each stage of the project

- The contract, in whatever form it is drawn up, formalizes the scope of work for a project

7.1   Know the Benefits of Understanding Financial Information

Just a few years ago, marketers had little interest or desire in knowing much about the financial side of a firm's business. Marketing was typically seen as a separate, independent discipline from business. A good marketer could turn up leads, research potential clients and help bring in (sometimes single-handedly) new business. SMPS broadened its vision to reflect that marketing involved more than just bringing in new business. It introduced the concept that the marketer should be aware of business and finance by bringing in projects that are profitable.

Why should a marketer be concerned with whether or not a potential project will be profitable? Isn't this the job of the technical staff, project managers and principals? On the outset, it may seem like marketing and finance are two distinct and separate disciplines, but in fact they are not. In well-run, cohesive and profitable firms, marketing and finance should be inseparable. Producing a profitable project may be heavily dependent on how well the technical staff performs their work. However, profitability can also be, at least in part, a function of the financial savvy of the marketer.

Consider the following: How financially solid is the client? How real is the project? Does it have funding? And is the client willing to pay a reasonable fee in a timely manner for services rendered? The marketer should be instrumental in helping to answer these questions, for example by checking a client's Dun & Bradstreet rating or talking with other firms that have worked for the client before.

Although it is possible for an excellent marketer to climb the corporate ladder to become a principal, that person becomes a lot more valuable to a firm and has many more options for personal growth if he or she understands the business and finance side of a firm.

 IDEA
Approach the review of financial information with a common-sense attitude. Financial information should be clear and understandable. Do not be afraid to ask questions regarding financial statements. A question often leads to a healthy discussion and leaves you better informed.

For some, the thought of reading and/or understanding financial statements may seem as complicated as understanding the detailed inner working of a personal computer or an automobile. Think of it this way: we probably all drive automobiles and operate computers. We can have varying levels of knowledge about how they operate and the principles behind them. As a marketer, you too can and should understand the basics of business and finance. The level of personal understanding you take on is up to you.

Reasons for marketers to expand their knowledge of financial principles include:

- **International work.** As we expand toward a global economy, there will be emerging opportunities that require a successful marketer to feel comfortable, not only in the business aspects of a local or regional economy, but also in dealing with foreign businesses where currency, operations and business approaches are different from what they are used to.

- **Company resource.** A marketer can be a more valuable resource to a firm's principals and management team if he or she can direct responsibility for the firm's profitability.

- **Personal growth and advancement.** Showing direct financial results (profitability) from one's activities is a strong motivator when one's performance is evaluated and when opportunities arise for advancement in a firm.

- **Training and education.** Learning financial business principles can help to prevent burnout by expanding one's perspective and developing new levels of interest, knowledge and talent.

- **Increased success.** The more understanding a marketer has of the firm's financial condition—for example, backlog, history of trends and paying clients—the more effective he or she will be in assessing which projects and clients to pursue. Without this kind of information, a marketer might continue to market an area which has historically been unprofitable for the firm.

Marketers have unique talents and personality traits that enable them to function well and perform in the business/financial community without having a degree in accounting. First of all, they know what's happening in the business world. In researching leads and potential business opportunities, they uncover new trends. They have the potential to meet and talk with lots of business people and they know how to ask questions. By the time a marketer passes a potential client to the proposal writers and technical staff, they probably know more about that prospective company than anyone else. The marketer should stay involved with the client during the duration of a project.

Remember, in a professional services organization, people really buy people—not firms or services. There are a number of logical and beneficial tasks that marketers can perform to stay in touch with the client and to help ensure that a project is satisfactory and profitable, which brings out the next unique characteristic of marketers—their people skills. Keeping in contact with the client seems only natural for the marketer who made the original contact. Maintaining client relations leads to the next project.

7.2   Learn the Basics

Business management is the area where most people would expect to discuss financial information. Financial information, however, is really only one part of an overall business continuum which should include marketing, business strategy, project management and accounting.

A firm's financial statement describes the financial condition of the company, including its profit or loss information. Before getting involved in the details of financial statements, there are a few rules of thumb in the form of ratios that are used by most professional services firms to get a quick picture of certain business parameters. The A/E/C industry has compiled statistics using these ratios, which are relatively easy and straightforward to understand. Marketers should grasp the concepts associated with these ratios.

7.2.1   Charge-Out Rate

All billable staff typically has an hourly charge-out rate that is used for the purpose of invoicing clients for time spent on projects. An individual's charge-out rate is based on their salary, the company's overhead (i.e., the cost of doing business) and the profit the company plans to make. Use the following formula to calculate the rate:

Staff hourly rate + (Staff hourly rate x Company overhead rate) + Profit =

Charge-out rate

Example: $40 + ($40 x 190 percent) + ($116 x 20 percent) = $139.20

7.2.2   Target Multiplier (aka Charge Multiplier)

The ratio of an employer's charge-out rate to his or her payroll rate is the target (or charge) multiplier. If someone is charged out at $140 per hour and paid a salary of $40 per hour, the charge multiplier is 3.5. It is not uncommon to leverage various charge multipliers in a firm, using lower multipliers for higher paid staff (principals) and higher multipliers for lower paid staff (production staff). A typical average rule of thumb for a

target multiplier is between 3.0 and 3.5. Here is how you'll calculate the target multiplier:

> **Charge-out rate / Staff hourly rate = Target multiplier**
>
> **Example: $140 / $40 = 3.5**

7.2.3 Net Multiplier

The net multiplier is the ratio of net revenues (generated by in-house labor only, without reimbursable expenses) to total direct labor (raw labor salary only, without any fringe benefits). If a firm's net revenues are $2,800,000 and its total direct labor expense charged to projects is $800,000, the net multiplier would be 3.50. This multiplier is what the firm actually achieved and is a measure of efficiency.

Clearly, a higher multiplier will lead to higher profits. Typical strategies to improve the net multiplier are to perform projects in your core expertise for a fixed fee, provide adequate employee software training and control unpaid scope creep. Calculate the net multiplier as follows:

> **Net revenue (in-house labor only) / Total direct labor (raw salary only) = Net multiplier**
>
> **Example: $2,800,000 / $800,000 = 3.5**

7.2.4 Overhead Rate

The overhead rate is the ratio of overhead costs—operating expenses not assigned to projects, including indirect salaries (labor that is not charged to projects)—to total direct labor (labor that is charged to projects). If a firm's overhead costs are $1,280,000 and its total direct labor is $800,000, the ratio would be 1.60 or 160 percent. This number can vary significantly depending on many factors particular to the firm. Values in the range of 125 to 200 percent, however, are common in the professional services industry.

Reasonable steps should be taken to control overhead costs. Typical strategies to control overhead are to reduce indirect labor (the largest component of overhead), obtain competitive quotes on insurance policies, and consolidate cell phone and other similar contracts into a single group contract. Here is an easy way to calculate the overhead rate:

Overhead costs (operating expenses, including indirect salaries) / Total direct labor = Overhead rate

Example: $1,280,000 / $800,000 = 1.60 or 160 percent

7.2.5 Staff Utilization Ratio

The staff utilization ratio is the ratio of a firm's total direct labor to its total labor (all salaries including fringe benefits). Another way that this ratio is sometimes calculated is based on the total hours charged to projects in relation to the total hours worked. This factor depicts how chargeable the company is and is related to the net effective multiplier. If a firm's direct labor is $800,000 and its total labor is $1,230,000, the ratio would be 65 percent. The industry standard is somewhere in the range of 60 to 65 percent.

A healthy staff utilization rate is perhaps the most important component of profitability. When utilization increases, it also has the benefit of decreasing the overhead rate, providing a double benefit. Strategies to increase the utilization rate include monitoring the utilization rate weekly and getting overhead employees chargeable to projects. Calculate the staff utilization ratio as follows:

Total direct labor / Total labor (all salaries and fringe benefits) = Staff utilization ratio

Example: $800,000 / $1,230,000 = 6.5 or 65 percent

7.2.6 Current Ratio

The current ratio is the ratio of the firm's current assets (for example: cash, accounts receivable, unbilled services, notes receivable, prepaid expenses) to its current liabilities (for example: accounts payable, advanced billings in excess of revenue, short-term notes payable, payroll, payroll taxes). If a firm has current assets of $1,040,000 and current liabilities of $300,000, the ratio is 3.47. A financially healthy firm will maintain a ratio of at least 2 to 1. Here is the current ratio calculation:

Current assets / Current liabilities = Current ratio

Example: $1,040,000 / $300,000 = 3.47

7.2.7 Net Profit Ratio

The net profit ratio is the ratio of net profit (income minus expenses) to net revenues. Depending on how one's firm is structured, the net profit ratio or percentage can vary depending on one's definition of revenue. It can be based on net (before) or

total (after) revenues. Pass-through items such as consultants and other reimbursable expenses, distribution of profit, bonus, and other discretionary items may be included or excluded. A firm's profit can vary, but let's all agree—it should be a positive number. The net profit ratio is calculated as follows:

Net profit (income − expenses) / Net revenue = Net profit ratio

7.2.8 Accounts Receivable Collections

The accounts receivable collections is the average number of days it takes to collect from clients for services (from the date of billing to the date of collection). First, it is necessary to determine the average day's sales by dividing 365 (days in a year) into the annual total revenues; then divide the average accounts receivable by the average day's sales. In the A/E/C industry, 60 to 65 days is common for accounts receivable collections. This descriptor affects cash flow. The longer it takes to collect monies due from invoices, the more interest a firm must pay to cover the monies it had to borrow to pay for the work already performed.

Slow collections falls squarely on the shoulders of the business side of a firm. Every effort should be made to invoice the client monthly—and as quickly as possible after month end. The invoice should be straightforward, easily understood by the client and free of mathematical errors, in order to avoid delays in payment. Use the following steps to calculate the accounts receivable figure:

Step 1: Total annual revenues / 365 (days in a year)
= Average day's sales

Step 2: Average accounts receivable / Average day's sales
= Accounts receivable

7.2.9 Financial Statements

Financial statements generally include a balance sheet and a profit/loss or revenue/ expense statement. In compiling these documents, the level of detail may seem overwhelming. There is a "generally accepted accounting principle" (GAAP) approach that outlines the procedure and format for preparing accounting information. Taken in its most basic form, marketers should realize that for A/E/C firms, income (or revenue) is generated almost exclusively by charging time to projects and collecting payments for the fees generated.

Expenses include all costs a firm expends in the process of doing business. Some costs are reimbursed by a client/project. Profit (i.e., revenues minus expenses) can be distributed by firm management as it sees fit. Bigger project budgets (or bigger proposals) don't necessarily mean more profit, especially if the projects are not managed properly. Any means by which expenses can be reduced could have a positive impact on bottom line profitability. Look for significant over or under amounts for income or expense categories, and request clarification.

7.2.10 Tracking Backlog

Backlog is defined as the work (revenue) logged which has yet to be completed. Backlog can be tracked via client type, when the work needs to be performed, and/or by dollars. Barring any unforeseen difficulty, a firm should be able to count on the revenue from this backlog in its long-term financial planning. It also will help to determine the potential HR requirements to perform the forthcoming work. A firm can use backlog to help plan for its future.

Decisions regarding potential growth can be supported by the amount of work a firm can be confident they have on the books. Tracking backlog should be done in conjunction with accounting, marketing and project management staff. Work with accounting staff in compiling the financial information, the numbers, the forms and the charts. Develop meaningful data that can be tracked easily and presented. Look for trends. The number (or percent) of proposals written, the number of projects won and the building sectors they came from are interesting indicators to monitor. The number of projects from new vs. existing or former clients is also informative to track. It is a well-known fact that it costs less to market existing clients than it does to find new clients.

Work with project managers and principals to let them know what you are tracking and why. Make sure that your firm is heading in the same direction and get their support and assistance. Your job will become easier as your associates work with you in tracking backlog.

7.3   Understand the Project Lifecycle

Most marketing philosophy assumes that the technical staff is responsible for a project once it's in the office. However, this is where the potential profits from a project can evaporate; marketers can be very instrumental during this time. You should stay involved during every phase of a project. Make sure that you know simple facts and critical issues about each project.

An occasional friendly call to the client emphasizes your firm's sincere interest in maintaining client contact. This contact measures the client's happiness with your firm's service. Some carefully asked questions such as, "How are we doing?" or "Is everything going OK with the project?" will probably quickly uncover any aspect of the project that needs attention. The information a client transmits to a marketer (assumed to be remote from the daily personalities involved in the project) could be very valuable to the project team and your firm's management.

Client relations need to be sold in-house and should be a team effort initiated by the marketer. The project manager should understand how the marketer can help keep the client happy and the project profitable throughout each of the following stages.

7.3.1 Getting the Project

The initiation stage of a project includes defining the scope, negotiating a fee and developing a contract. We'll discuss this in more detail later on in the section, so for now here are a few questions to consider during this stage:

- What is the basic scope of the project?
- What is the anticipated value of the contract?
- What type of contract is it?
- What are the key schedule/performance dates?
- Who are the key players for the client, your firm and consultants?

Failing to define the exact nature of the project and plan its completion with the appropriate level of detail puts your firm at risk of not understanding, and therefore not meeting, your client's needs.

7.3.2 Doing the Project

The execution stage involves the management of resources (e.g., money, people, time, materials, etc.) to ensure that deliverables are executed according to plan. This includes monitoring obstacles and risks so that any issues can be corrected before they get out of control. The ultimate goal is to make sure that the project stays on track. Check in with the project's activities often. Where are we now? Does that align with the project plan? What should be completed at this point? Is it? If you notice that the project is falling behind, or an unforeseen problem has arisen, finding out early will give you more time to take corrective action. Quality assessment and control should be measured now as well.

During this stage, the scope of work you'd previously worked out with the client may change. This is a normal part of the construction process, as designs may need to be modified based on site conditions, the availability of materials, changes requested by a contractor, etc. Keep a record of the changes made (once you've determined they're possible) and make the necessary adjustments to the contract. If the client requests additional work that falls outside of the original project scope, you may need to renegotiate fees as well.

7.3.3 Finishing the Project

Once the project has been completed, the contracts associated with the project should be formally closed following the resolution of any items still open. Afterwards, conduct a project review. What did the project team learn from experiences that they can apply to future projects? What went well? What went badly, and why?

Don't forget to get feedback from your client as well. Conducting debriefing interviews, also called client reviews, are an investment in your relationship with your client. In these private meetings, you can learn your client's impressions of your performance, as well as their perceptions of your image and reputation.

Clients are most receptive to debriefing interviews at their offices and at their convenience. The interviews are most effective when conducted in person, but they may take place over the phone. Whether conducted by a trained team member or an outside consultant, it is the interviewer's responsibility to build an atmosphere of trust and open dialogue. Set the tone by demonstrating friendliness and a willingness to listen with an accepting attitude.

 TARGET POINT
The critical task is to pose open-ended questions in a manner that encourages complete answers. Taking notes during the discussion shows the client that such feedback is deemed worthy of further consideration.

To reinforce the position of listener, end the debriefing session by asking, "Is there anything else you'd like to tell me?" When the client has finished, offer assurance that any shortcomings mentioned will be dealt with. This is not the time to insert a sales pitch. Remember that this is a time of learning; clients will be more open and offer more information when they're confident that there's no sales pressure. Be sure to thank the client for taking the time to provide honest, informative answers.

7.4   Understand Basic Contract Principles

Agreements involving design professionals in the construction industry range from the simple to the complex. Generally, the type and complexity of the professional service contract is dictated by the size and scope of the project, as well as the range of services to be performed by the design professional. You should strive to reach an agreement that clearly defines:

- Responsibilities on the project
- Responsibilities of the party with whom it is contracting
- The specific scope of its work
- Compensation for services, including additional services and whether reimbursable expenses will be recovered
- The time period in which the work should be performed
- Under what conditions the relationship may be terminated

Likewise, in any agreement, you should attempt to balance the risks inherent in providing your firm's services on the project with its obligations under the agreement. In other words, only agree to be responsible for the things that you can control. Finally, you should strive to enter into agreements that are clear, concise and unambiguous, so as to avoid disputes at a later date concerning the language of its agreement.

This section is intended to provide a general overview of contract formation principles, various contract forms that are used by design professionals on construction projects and specific contract provisions that are often used in contracts.

So, what is a contract? A contract is an exchange of promises between two or more parties that creates a legal obligation between them. For example, one party agrees to provide a certain service; the other party agrees to pay a certain amount for that service. The following terms help demonstrate how a contract works at a basic level.

- An "offer" occurs when a party offers to perform a service or provide a good in exchange for certain consideration, or when a party offers to pay a certain amount in exchange for receiving a service or a good. An offer that is limited as to the length of time it will remain open for acceptance is called a "firm offer."

- A party "accepts" an offer when it agrees to provide a service or exchange certain consideration for the service. A party may accept an offer by simply engaging in the performance of the service that is requested. A response to an offer that varies the terms of the offer is deemed to be a counter-proposal or counter-offer and is not an acceptance of the offer. (It is then up to the original offerer to decide whether it wants to accept the counter-offer on the same terms as proposed or make its own counter-offer.)

- Consideration is defined as the value exchanged between the two parties in a contract. It can consist of promises, services, goods and/or money.

A properly prepared contract is critical to the avoidance of disputes and in identifying the rights and obligations of the parties to the transaction. Obtaining legal advice from a knowledgeable attorney is also extremely important to ensuring that a contract is properly prepared. Using a contract "form" without tailoring it to your specific needs and the specific project can lead to significant problems.

The purpose of all contracts are: (a) to appropriately allocate the risk between parties, (b) to avoid ambiguity in connection with the material obligations and responsibilities between the parties, and (c) to establish timelines and compensation. As long as these requirements are met, the contract itself can take a few different forms. A contract might be oral, as in an exchange of verbal promises, or written down in either a standard form or customized document.

The following provisions should be included in any contract:

- **Scope of work.** A detailed description of the scope of services you will perform.

- **Obligations of the design professional.** Details concerning the responsibilities you hold in the performance of your services, including the standard of care to be used to measure your services and your obligation to review and abide by laws, codes and regulations that concern the project.

- **Responsibilities of the owner.** Details concerning the obligations that the owner has to your firm, including an overall budget for the project and evidence of the owner's financial stability.

- **Construction cost.** A definition of what constitutes the "construction cost" of the work.

- **Ownership and use of documents.** Confirm that your architects' drawings, specifications and other documents are to be used solely for the project at hand.

- **Alternate dispute resolution.** Consider whether you want to include procedures in your agreement detailing alternative ways to resolve disputes (e.g., mediation or arbitration).

- **Architect as arbitrator.** A provision found is many standard form contracts makes you the initial decider of disputes that arise on the project. Make sure that you clarify your role in arbitrating these disputes.

- **Waiver of consequential damages.** Any damages that are not directly caused by a breach of contract, but may result from it, including home office overhead, loss profits and the like.

- **Limitation of liability.** A provision that defines and limits the types and amount of damages for which you can be held responsible.

- **Termination of services.** A definition of under what circumstances either you or the owner/client may terminate the services.

 7.5 Key Terms

Below are the main terms covered in this section:

- Charge-out rate
- Target multiplier
- Net Multiplier
- Overhead rate
- Staff utilization ratio
- Current ratio
- Net profit ratio
- Accounts receivable collections
- Financial statement
- Backlog
- Firm offer
- Consideration
- Contract
- Scope of work
- Mediation
- Arbitration
- Consequential damages

8   Promote a Firm-Wide BD Culture

A company's BD culture is key to its success in today's highly competitive environment. There are various models that can be used to understand, and strengthen, a firm's BD culture; and there are ways to enhance the contribution to the culture that various players within the organization play.

By the end of this section, you should understand the following key points, and be able to use them in the management of your marketing group:

- How BD culture can be better understood in light of various models, and these same models can be used to strengthen the culture
- Rainmakers thrive within healthy BD cultures
- BD culture is defined and expressed across all levels of the organization

8.1   Develop and Implement Strategies to Advance a BD Culture

In a volatile economy, any number of factors (e.g., changes in legislation, significant increases in construction material or operational costs or lack of funding) can trigger swift changes in the "normal" way of conducting daily business practices–changes that lend themselves to a shaky trust in future growth. These concerns, coupled with the daily struggles of financial prudence, long-term viability and community involvement, are the challenges that continue to plague leaders in federal, state and local organizations; as well as in private industry.

It comes as no surprise then that, as clients try to squeeze dollars out of pennies, the opportunities for consultants to win new work are even more competitive. For firms to continue to increase their backlogs, "business as usual" no longer applies. In order to overcome commoditization and maintain profitability, firms must provide value-based services and differentiate from their competitors.

Firms must be smarter and more adaptable in a dynamic business climate. Each and every pursuit must begin with effective pre-positioning–getting to know the client and the project and letting the client get to know you. That means that each BD opportunity must yield knowledgeable pursuit information. For most firms, this shift in the corporate approach to pursuing work results in a fundamental shift in philosophy– one that establishes a BD culture.

What exactly is a BD culture? First, let's define BD as "the gathering and compilation of client and pursuit knowledge in advance of a request for proposals through direct interaction with the client." The key to this definition is "direct" interaction. Marketing, on the other hand, is defined as "indirect" interaction with the client. This means that, initially, you meet with the client to understand their organization without "selling" your services.

IDEA

As your relationship with the client develops, begin to inquire about future opportunities for work. This initiates a second round of interviews with the client selection committee and/or project shareholders to identify the project issues and hot buttons for the individual selection committee members.

Three elements—the process, the system/database and training—are essential for developing a BD culture. The BD process is how you conduct BD. The BD system or database is where you capture and manage your information. Training is how you educate your employees on the BD process and the system.

With leadership embracing a BD culture, everyone becomes responsible for winning work. A BD culture is an investment in company growth that takes time to create the process, develop the database and train employees with the simple goal of winning more work, more efficiently.

8.2 Understand Models of BD Cultures

Managers of professional firms know the problem. They encourage their people to become rainmakers, but after a few limp efforts to bring in business, most give up. Those who run the firm are likely to conclude that rainmakers are born and not made. They, too, give up on their efforts to teach people to make rain. Why are many professionals so quick to give up their efforts to bring in business, and what can you do about it?

Curiously, few are defeated by the market, which would reward them if they kept selling. They just stop trying. Why? Certainly not because they are fools or wimps. To the contrary, most are smart people and tough enough to push themselves and others to the limit to satisfy a client. Nor is it because they are hopelessly unskilled. A few may be, but others, who have solid interpersonal skills and may even have received sales training, give up just as quickly. Why? To solve this problem and learn how to create rainmakers, you must understand the process of BD and sales, and establish a realistic set of stages for this process at your own firm.

8.2.1 Valley of Death

Research shows that giving up usually results from a misfit between the way professionals manage projects and the way sales grow. Most professionals see the relationship between hours worked on a project and results as linear (see the figure below). Three hours of effort should produce three hours of results. Young professionals learn early to work hard and to avoid a conversation with a project manager that begins, "You've spent a week on this, and I don't see a week's worth of result."

CLIENT WORK AND
SALES DEVELOP BY
DIFFERENT LOGICS

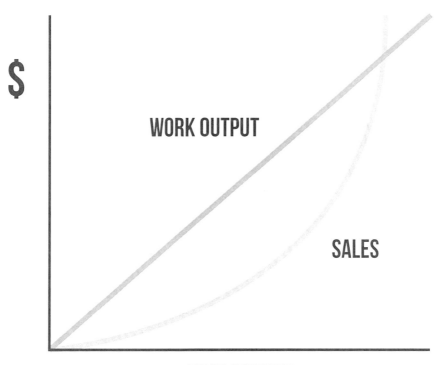

Figure 8.1 - Client Work and Sales Develop by Different Logics (Marketing Handbook)

When a professional begins to develop business, he or she approaches the effort with the same mentality: an hour's effort should produce an hour of result. But client development doesn't work that way. Instead, it grows much the way a steady annual investment grows at a fixed interest rate. At first there is little, if any, result from the time spent. Later, small results may come, but they seem minuscule and a scant return on all the effort invested. During this period, seasoned project managers who aspire to be rainmakers may even see their performance in other areas decline. They may, for example, manage fewer projects because they are diverting time to client development. This deeply discouraging period is the "Valley of Death," from which few professionals emerge as rainmakers. Most rededicate themselves to those activities where they perceive that they get a higher return on the time they invest—e.g., project work.

Firm management often contributes to this problem by pressuring professionals to bring in business when there is an urgent need, but tolerating inattention to BD when times are good. This reinforces the impression that BD efforts are expected to bring in work quickly, and that results will come even if effort is turned on and off periodically. That simply isn't the way it works.

Somehow, true rainmakers have learned that client development requires long-term and continuous effort. Kenneth Diehl of Smith Seckman Reid, Inc. in Nashville, TN, remembers being told early in his career that it takes one to three years to develop a relationship that will bring in business. Over the years, he has found this to be true. The late Norman Kurtz, founder of Flack + Kurtz of New York, describes an even longer development cycle which many rainmakers have benefited from. He says, "In your 20s, 30s and 40s, you have to develop a lot of relationships with people you work with. Some will make it big and some won't, but by the time you are older, some can give you work."

8.2.2   Sales Success Cycle

The few professionals who persist at client development, as these two rainmakers did, learn that success grows geometrically. A slow start is natural and is often followed by small success that leads to sudden and substantial sales growth. Your challenge is to get professionals through the Valley of Death to the stage where success feeds itself. Once there, professionals enter the Sales Success Cycle, shown in the figure below. Success builds self-confidence, which gives them the self-motivation to work through the many small setbacks inevitable in selling until they succeed again. Once in the cycle, few ever leave it.

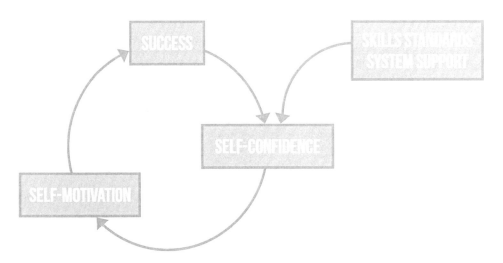

Figure 8.2 - The Sales Success Cycle (Marketing Handbook)

Professionals can enter the cycle at any point. Ford Harding, the founding principal of Harding & Company, has authored two books on rainmaking (see Related Resources for more information) and emphasizes that his company's database of rainmakers has examples of people entering at each of the three points on the cycle. A few have early, lucky success that convinces them they can bring in business. Shortly after taking her first job, one of the people Harding interviewed went to a party at a neighbor's. There she met the head of a local college who hired her firm. After that, she just kept selling.

Others seem to have always enjoyed the self-confidence that carries them through the early stages of client development, when results are slim. As Ron Schmidt, founder of the New Jersey architectural firm of Ronald Schmidt & Associates, says, "I've been influenced by positive-thinking people all my life. Marketing is about attitude. When you read books about great salespeople, it's all about attitude. They never give up. You have to put the fear aside and go ahead."

8.2.3   Rainmaking System

The management of a professional firm must help its people enter the Sales Success Cycle at one of these three points. Harding recommends a four-part intervention process which gives professionals the following four "S"s.

8.2.3.1 Skills

Your professionals will need skills to succeed at selling. Above all else, they need good questioning skills. Most have a mistaken belief that selling equals talking. They feel that they must tell a prospective client about past projects and about the firm's ability to solve problems. Left to their own devices, many will talk themselves right out of winning a project. Sales training will help build better habits. If your people are likely to give presentations, training in that area is also valuable. This is where most firms begin and end their efforts to create rainmakers.

But skills training alone will not see your people through; the slow rate at which business first develops doesn't result from an absence of skills. It is a natural phenomenon that the accomplished project manager understands neither logically nor emotionally. Here are some additional tools you can use to help your aspiring rainmakers through the Valley of Death.

8.2.3.2 Standards

The sense of failure that professionals in the Valley of Death feel results from applying project management standards to client development, where they cause great harm. For example, it is so unusual to call an active client six times and not receive a return call that it would be reasonable for a project manager to feel concerned should this occur. But if you call a former client with whom you haven't spoken for several years, it can take many calls to get through. These are different situations requiring different reactions. When developing business, there are many such small judgements that will be in error if they are made on the basis of standards developed managing projects.

Cumulatively, they will discourage an aspiring rainmaker and increase the chances that he or she will give up.

There are several things you can do to recalibrate professionals' expectations, including:

- Emphasize building relationships that will foster new business throughout a career rather than focusing on sales now. Professionals are often reluctant to make calls because they believe that the people they know won't react favorably to a sales call. Usually, they're right. As Leonard Koven, a founder of Atkinson Koven Feinberg LLP of New York, says, "If you want people to call you, call them first. I don't just call to get business. I call people when there is no project at stake, just to say hello, see how things are going, and talk about friends we have in common." Develop good relationships with buyers and referrers, and work will follow.

- Help your aspiring rainmakers develop the appropriate discipline. Specific disciplines include meeting new people, making calls and having meetings with people they already know. A true rainmaker will make a minimum of 25 calls a week to develop relationships and pursue business. This number is far out of reach for most of your people; many will find it difficult to draw up a list of 25 people to call even once. In such cases, they need to meet more people. There are opportunities all around them on their projects. There are owners, developers, engineers and architects, real estate brokers and others.

- At one firm Harding interviewed, young professionals are expected to collect five new business cards a month. This will add roughly 50 people to their contact lists each year, of whom five are likely to be keepers. The professionals are then asked to make periodic calls to the people whose cards they have collected. By the time a professional has been with the firm for five years, he or she will have relationships with 25 true players in the marketplace, and additional relationships with others who may be helpful.

8.2.3.3 Systems

Harding's interviews with more than 100 rainmakers show that virtually all maintain the call and meeting discipline required to bring in business by working a system. The system dictates what they need to do at any given time and holds their feet to the fire. Give most professionals 15 minutes to do some marketing, and most will use up the time just figuring out what to do. Give 15 minutes to a rainmaker, and he or she will know just what to do because the system dictates what calls need to be made or letters written.

The exact nature of the system varies from rainmaker to rainmaker, but all work a system. A system is a dynamically linked set of processes. A generic diagram of a rainmaking system is shown below. Boxes represent processes and arrows are the linkages between processes. Both are important.

A RAINMAKING SYSTEM

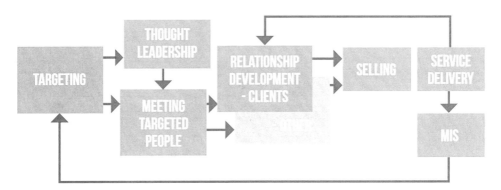

Figure 8.3 - A Rainmaking System (Marketing Handbook)

Usually the processes for meeting people and developing relationships drive the rest of the system. Elements in these processes often include:

- **Call and meeting quotas.** Rainmakers are always on the phone and out meeting people, because they understand the most basic rule of selling—you will never sell anything unless you talk to people.

- **Contact tracking.** The development of this has been greatly eased by the emergence of contact management software.

- **Processes for meeting new people to add to the contact base.** Examples include actively participating in professional associations, running seminars, working for charities and participating in formal networking groups.

TARGET POINT

A System Based on Associations

Judy Nitsch, founder of Judith Nitsch Engineering, Inc. of Boston, has built much of her business through relationships developed by working with colleagues in professional organizations. She has been a member of SMPS, the Boston Society of Civil Engineers, American Consulting Engineers Council and New England Women in Real Estate. She picked these organizations because the members include prospective clients and other worthwhile contacts.

When Nitsch joins a group, she volunteers to work in it actively. That way, she gets to work with the other members and gets to know them as people. She finds that they are more likely to give or refer work to her if they have seen her in action in an association. If you are competent at volunteer work, Nitsch believes, they know you will be conscientious as a paid consultant.

Nitsch always tries to have association meetings in her firm's offices to show that her firm is real and substantial. Her firm makes sure that their offices look good for those meetings. People who come say, "I didn't know you had so many people," and "You have better computers than we have." That makes an impression and, as a result, it helps some of them become clients.

Association work gives her the chance to meet people, it helps her get to know them and it helps structure her marketing efforts, so that she stays in touch and visible.

Key Concepts for this Story:
- Active membership in a professional organization can provide many ways to showcase your own talents
- Volunteering and helping others in a group of like-minded professionals can lead to unexpected business opportunities

Every rainmaker has a system, and each system looks different. Helping each of your would-be rainmakers develop a system that works for him or her is a key part of the staff development effort.

At a firm level, you also need to make sure that your compensation system is aligned to the client development behaviors you want to encourage. During the first year that aspiring rainmakers work at client development, cash incentives may not be appropriate, but there are other things you can do, including providing them a modest budget for client development or praising actions that will lead to work later.

Management should also make sure that the marketing organization runs smoothly in support of the professionals' client development efforts. The professionals need to be able to get out emails and other marketing documents efficiently. They need to be able to invite their contacts to firm marketing events.

8.2.3.4 Support

Compared to project management, client development is an emotional rollercoaster. The uncertainty of turning an initial contact into a client can give a professional a feeling of complete loss of control, and professionals, like most people, like to feel in control of their own fates. Cheering them when they win and helping them see loss as simply a necessary step to winning that same client at some future time are critical management responsibilities. More subtly, a principal showing interest and enthusiasm for the project manager's client development efforts week in and week out—even when the principal is busy and distracted by other things—will contribute to the manager's success. With some people, good-natured nagging may also help.

Emotional support is a critical part of the mentoring required to create rainmakers. This support is particularly important while professionals are in the Valley of Death and see little return on their marketing efforts. Many of the rainmakers in Harding's survey commented on how important support was to their success. Both A. Eugene Kohn,

founder of Kohn Pedersen Fox Associates PC, and Tom Bathgate, one of the owners of PWI Engineering, remember the support they received from the architect, Vincent Kling, a highly dramatic and successful rainmaker, early in their careers.

Much hinges on the development of rainmakers: your success in the next downturn, the sustainability of your profits when an aging rainmaker retires and your ability to build new practices and open new offices. In some cases, the very survival of the firm is contingent on the rainmaker's success. Everyone could benefit from paying more attention to helping aspiring rainmakers cross the Valley of Death.

8.2.4 Performing BD during Project Execution

A principal or business developer is responsible for obtaining new clients for their firm—i.e., for winning their first project with a new client. Once a firm begins working with a new client, the project team is responsible for keeping that client. The actions of the firm's project team during that project will control whether the firm gets (or loses) an opportunity for the client's next project. The project team is also in the best position to help identify additional project opportunities with their new client.

The principal or business developer certainly has an important role in obtaining repeat work from current clients, but the project staff—especially the project manager—are the ones who really have direct control based on their ongoing project activities and communications skills. Contrary to what some may think, the BD professionals and marketing department staff can't control the project team's BD actions during project execution, but they can help facilitate further BD with that client.

A key factor in retaining clients in professional service firms is client satisfaction. This requires a firm to forge a strong connection with the client; understand the client's personality, goals, objectives and expectations; incorporate them into an A/E/C's firm's plan for serving that client; and constantly identify opportunities to improve the quality of service that clients experience.

And then it dawned on firms that, in their efforts to market themselves and develop new business, they had lost sight of the most important—and constant—factor in the equation of success: the client. Thus began a renewed focus on "client satisfaction" and on building strong relationships to get the next project.

There is little argument that client satisfaction is a key factor in client retention efforts of professional service firms. The mantra has become, "Do a good job, and clients will be happy and return to us with future work; they will be loyal." Yet, A/E/C firms need to be mindful that client retention is complex and that it is a critical success factor.

IDEA

Frederick Reichheld, in The Loyalty Effect, writes:

"Customer retention has three dimensions—customer loyalty, employee loyalty and investor loyalty. Loyalty has implications that extend to every corner of every business system that seeks the benefit of steady customers. Retention is not simply one more operating statistic; it is the central gauge that integrates all the dimensions of a business and measures how well the firm is creating value for its customers."

Research into customer satisfaction and loyalty (retention) indicates that client satisfaction does not guarantee loyalty; it is driven by four factors:

1. **Needs/values fit.** The extent to which the client's needs and values are satisfied in your dealings with them (responsiveness, access, services, performance, results).

2. **Involvement.** The extent to which the client was involved with you before, during and after your dealings with them (input, communication, decision-making).

3. **Disposition to alternatives.** The extent of the attraction the client feels toward competitors.

4. **Depth of ambivalence.** The extent to which the attraction to alternatives creates indecision about which to choose.

Of these four factors, you have the ability to control two: the needs/values fit and your involvement with the clients. Your clients want to be engaged by and with you. When asked in surveys to describe what makes a service firm stand out in their mind, the responses by many client representatives repeat common themes:

- "I want firms that respect my experience and knowledge (related to my responsibilities), and that respond with solutions which meet my objectives (not theirs)."

- "I want firms that do not walk away after the project is done (after they have my business)."

- "I want firms that make themselves accessible to me to answer questions and give me help when I need it, even if I have no project (work) for them."

- "I want consultants to spend their time figuring out how they can help me do my job better and how to keep me informed about things of value to me without wasting my time."

Professional expertise and doing a good job—in and of themselves—do not impress clients; that's what they expected when they hired an A/E/C firm. A client's basic expectation is that a firm will do a good job providing the services promised and

that the results will be what the client wanted. What makes your firm a hero with satisfied clients is the way in which your firm provides its services and how your firm's employees connect with and engage the client over and above the service itself. The single most effective link to future work is the person-to-person connection made with clients before, during and following a project.

8.2.5 Building Relationships

Building enduring relationships with others is a complex process that involves a range of philosophical, ethical, practical and emotional issues. The process typically takes place over a period of time, during which both parties are constantly evaluating—objectively and subjectively—how well they connect in terms of these critical issues, as well as their general interests.

Blackridge, Ltd. developed the Curve of Relationships© (shown in the figure below) as a model from which to describe and discuss the relationship-building process. The curve can best be understood by thinking about your closest personal (non-professional) relationship (spouse, partner, fiancée, mentor, school chum or whomever) and how that close relationship developed over time.

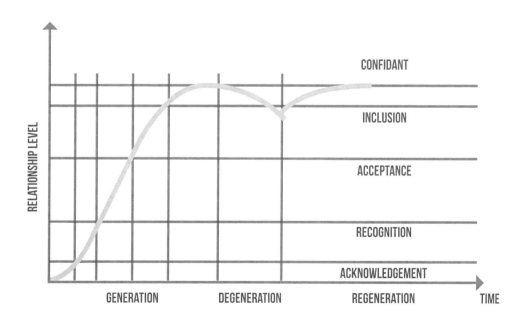

Figure 8.4 - Curve of Relationships (Marketing Handbook)

As the curve illustrates, one can recognize at least four, and perhaps five, specific levels of connection that were achieved as the relationship matured, and three separate phases of evolution. Those five levels are as follows:

1. **Acknowledgment.** The first meeting/introduction, following which basic information is exchanged.

2. **Recognition.** Subsequent encounters, casual or arranged (a.k.a. "dates"), at which mutual recall of previous conversations and mutual understanding of respective interests, skills and capabilities occurs.

3. **Acceptance.** Recognition of similar interests, values, ethics and philosophies where an initial level of trust exists and one is invited into the "outer circle" of acquaintances and colleagues.

4. **Inclusion.** Recognition that interests, values, ethics and philosophies are the same; the level of "trust" has increased; one becomes part of the "inner circle" of friends and colleagues; one is privy to information others are not.

5. **Confidant.** Achievement of a high level of trust; one is perceived as true advisor; highly personal; one is sought out for advice/counsel; willingness/ability to be a resource; one can confront issues directly and is unafraid to speak up.

In an ideal world, all relationships would develop smoothly and continuously from the initial meeting (the Acknowledgment level) through Inclusion to Confidant. Unfortunately, the world is not always ideal; not all relationships develop smoothly or continuously. Sometimes when the parties disagree or they are out of contact and the relationship begins to degenerate, a period of recovery is required. The relationship curve can, and usually does, involve three phases of evolution, which are defined as:

1. **Generation.** Movement up the curve from Acknowledgment to Confidant.

2. **Degeneration.** That point at which a relationship begins to falter and break down; it can occur at any time and for any reason if you are not alert.

3. **Regeneration.** The intense effort required to reverse degeneration of the relationship and move back up the curve.

Development of a professional or business relationship proceeds in the same fashion as a personal relationship. By understanding the five levels and three phases of the Curve of Relationships, you can identify where you are in your business relationships and work to move to the next level.

One way for a firm to be effective at this is to use the zipper effect: pair people at your firm to those in like positions at the client's firm up and down the chain of command. Having only one person in your firm know one person at the client firm is a recipe for disaster. What happens if one of them leaves their firm? Your firm's relationship with that client will go with it.

Here are several examples of pieces of the zipper for a structural firm: the president should know the president or branch office manager of their architect clients; department managers should be friendly with the studio design head; the marketing manager should know the architecture firm's marketing manager; the project engineer should be on a first-name basis with the client's architectural staff, etc. Of course, the BD people at each firm should know each other and collaborate often!

8.2.6 Internal Marketing Examples

Internal marketing is what service firms do to train and motivate client-contact employees and support staff to work as a team to provide client satisfaction. In short, internal marketing's sole focus is on the people inside a firm—the people who deliver the work and service the clients. Internal marketing fosters training and motivation of employees—principally those with client contact, but support employees as well. It requires leadership, direction, planning and constant attention. Internal marketing is as central to a firm's survival as is external marketing—focused as it is on the clients, prospects, referral sources, consultants, vendors and suppliers outside a firm.

The best firms in the design and construction industry execute some kind of internal marketing. Each one does it differently and at their own pace. In this section, we will highlight firms that have successfully used internal marketing to help them mobilize a collective team effort to grow their firm's business. (See section 2 for a review of how to develop an internal marketing communications system.)

The following examples describe the ways in which some notable firms have kept their staff motivated, trained, informed, recognized and rewarded through exceptional internal marketing efforts:

- Gensler is an international architecture, interiors, planning and consulting firm with 46 offices. The firm offered incentives to employees by awarding bonuses twice a year. One bonus was generally based on individual performance, while the other was based on the performance of the specific office and the overall firm. To personalize the occasion, a letter from founder Art Gensler accompanied each bonus check and/or a meeting with the office's managing principal was held. Gensler also conducted weekly conference calls among all offices, produced an online newsletter every two weeks, and sent a monthly newsletter to all employees.

- C.H. Guernsey & Company is a diversified professional consulting firm. Once per year, they flew everyone to Virginia for a variety of internal marketing activities, including teambuilding exercises.

- HNTB is a national architecture, planning and engineering company with 60 offices nationwide. They individualized a "career development planning process" for each employee that was tied to the firm's overall strategic plan. They also conducted an ongoing training program called "Common Denominators for Success" that emphasized best practices, so everyone in the firm would know what they are.

- Mulvanny G2 Architecture is an international architecture firm with five offices worldwide. They presented the "Marketing Shark Award" to non-principals who brought in good leads. The shark was a $10 plastic pool toy, about five feet long, and the recipient hung it above their cubicle until it passed to the next recipient. Before passing it on, they signed and dated it. The presentation of this award was announced by the Jaws theme song during a staff meeting, and the shark was lowered into the crowd. It also awarded the "Golden Tuba" to market leaders for hitting their marketing plan goals and client targets.

Internal marketing is the next, exciting frontier for professional services marketing. It is a multi-dimensional strategy for growing a firm from the inside out. Its focus is on the people inside a firm. It is a continuous, participative process that fosters training and motivation of employees—principally those with client contact, although executives and support employees are also included. Effective internal marketing requires leadership, direction and planning. It is targeted primarily to the people who perform technical services—mobilizing their energies and motivating their pursuit of shared goals (and rewards).

8.3 Define Roles, Responsibilities and Training across Firm

BD is a continuous, ongoing process involving everyone in the firm. While the need for a strong BD effort to acquire work is generally acknowledged as important, too often the need to maintain that strong effort is forgotten once a project is underway. This section will focus on the importance of BD during project execution to establish strong client relationships, and the critical role of the principals, business developers, marketing staff and the project team in that effort.

8.3.1 Marketers

Chiefly responsible for developing internal markets are marketing professionals, whose various roles are outlined in detail in section 1. These roles range from chief marketing officers, marketing principals, directors, and managers to marketing coordinators, assistants and specialists. Business developers, as well as the communications, public relations and graphics staff, can also contribute to the internal marketing program.

While the focus of their efforts will vary from internal to external markets, marketers—whatever their specific responsibility—function primarily as catalysts. They make things happen. They generate results. They orchestrate the effort to secure and retain external as well as internal clients. They lead the efforts to train and motivate their in-house colleagues to work as a team.

Marketers play many positions on a firm's marketing team, alternating as coaches, quarterbacks, cheerleaders or support. Their responsibilities can range just as widely. As William L. Peel, Jr., AIA, an executive with Marshall Erdman & Associates, puts it, "Marketers get their strokes from the firm's collective successes. They build other people's reputations in support of the firm's overall strategic goals. Rarely in the limelight, they focus the spotlights and flip all the switches."

Marketers are catalysts in developing both external and internal markets. Three typical internal markets include:

- Technical staff (discipline leaders to junior staff)
- Executive and senior managers (principals, owners, senior officers)
- Nontechnical support staff (administrative, clerical, corporate support personnel)

The marketer's work—now referred to as the business developer's work—does not end with the award of a project. In fact, some firms expect their business developers to be involved in the active management of key clients, as the account manager/project executive. This expanded role for the business developer may be project-focused (i.e., one-time) or for the long term. Most typically, it is employed for clients with whom the firm expects to have an extended working relationship and it is intended to strengthen and support the project team's relationship with the client and provide continuity for the firm over the longer term.

Whether or not the account manager/project executive role is an official responsibility for the business developer within a firm, he or she should assume one or more of five distinct roles during project execution. These roles are as follows.

8.3.1.1 Interpreter

As a result of the strong relationships developed with clients prior to the awarding of a project, many business developers develop a solid understanding of the client's personality, goals and objectives. In addition, during the pre-award period, the business developer is also instrumental in creating the environment which establishes (positively or negatively) the client's expectations.

Therefore, the first important role of the business developer is that of interpreter, as they play an important part in the following three areas:

1. Selecting the project team—including subconsultants as appropriate—and matching to the extent possible what they know of the client's personality with the appropriate personalities of the firm

2. Interpreting the client's goals, objectives and expectations for the project team and ensuring the team understands and incorporates them into the project approach

3. Translating the client's goals, objectives and expectations into the proposal and interview through to the final contractual agreement between the parties

8.3.1.2 Advocate/Mediator

As the individual who best understands the client's personality, goals, objectives and expectations, the business developer can be an objective link between the client and the project team. He or she is the client's alter-ego within the project team and the next-to-last point of last resort (principals should be the point of last resort). In this capacity, they should be continuously aware of project status vis-à-vis the client's goals, objectives and expectations.

Can this be accomplished? Yes, and here are three suggestions that will facilitate participation and minimize disruption of schedules and routines.

1. **Periodically attend regular in-house project team meetings (depending on project size and schedule, probably at least monthly).** Consult with the project team leader to have client service issues included as the first item on every meeting agenda. Be prepared with questions about issues or concerns that might interfere with the team's ability to meet the client's goals, objectives and expectations; press discussion as to how the team intends to resolve those issues or concerns.

2. **Depending on the project's size and schedule, attend at least one project team meeting each quarter with the client.** Observe and assess the dynamics between the client and the team (e.g., communication, personalities, etc.). Verify that the client's goals, objectives and expectations are being met. As follow up to this meeting, provide useful feedback to team members that can help enhance their skills and keep the project team focused on the client.

3. **Independently maintain personal contact with the client as the firm's ombudsman.** The opportunity afforded by these one-on-one meetings can be invaluable to the firm and its relationship with the client. Listen objectively to the client's experiences with the firm and the project team; avoid becoming defensive or pointing fingers. The goal is to learn of issues (e.g., project performance, billing, responding to questions) which may not have been communicated to or heard by the firm or the project team.

 TARGET POINT
As the advocate for the client, voice any concerns immediately to the appropriate individual(s) within the firm or team. If a client is experiencing problems or has concerns with any aspect of the project and cannot find solutions, the business developer should become the mediator and help find satisfactory resolution that is in the best interests of all parties.

8.3.1.3 Coach

Another outcome of the business developer's advocate/mediator role is that they can serve as a coach for other staff. In this capacity, business developers can provide "real-time" support to staff by adopting the "lessons learned" approach in their involvement with clients and the project teams during a project. To be effective in this role as coach, the business developer must have good interpersonal skills and sensitivity to how individuals react and respond to suggestions and critique.

Through the lessons-learned process, the business developer can use actual project situations as coaching opportunities to develop and enhance the skills of both principals and staff in a variety of critical areas, including improving interpersonal and client relations, responding to and resolving conflict, running effective meetings and presenting difficult information.

Depending on the specific situation and personalities involved, this coaching role can be carried out either through one-on-one interaction or small group activity or through a more structured internal or external professional development program.

8.3.1.4 Contributor

The particular skills and background a business developer possesses (be they marketing, finance, public relations, communications, advertising or technical) can be transformed into a valuable service to assist clients in a variety of ways during a project. The opportunities are limited only by time, resources, creativity and understanding (or lack thereof) of the client's business and needs.

The job of the business developer is to develop that understanding and identify opportunities that will maximize their potential for contribution to a successful project and client relationship that makes sense for the firm. Examples of how some business developers have used their skills to support a client during a project include the following (note that some may even be considered billable time):

1. **Helping prepare documents for and participating in public hearings to help clients obtain permits and funding approvals.** Examples include public facility funding (bond issue campaigns), siting/zoning issues or environmental permits.

2. **Preparing materials to help the client fund, market or sell the project.** Examples include potential donors for a university building, tenants of a high-end office space, residents of a retirement/congregate care facility for seniors, healthcare providers for patient care/treatment centers or students in a college recruitment brochure featuring specialized learning spaces.

3. **Preparing materials for and/or arranging and participating in special events.** Examples include preparing press releases for community outreach programs; helping to organize groundbreaking, topping-off, and ribbon-cutting ceremonies; or participating in special fund-raising events for projects or client-supported charitable organizations.

4. **Using a specialized non-design/construction background to the client's benefit.** Examples include a financial background to perform pro-forma cash flow analyses of project scenarios for a development project, an introduction to your banker to help a client arrange financing for a new project, or an educational background to assist a client in the training of staff.

8.3.1.5 Nudge

This is perhaps the business developer's most unique role because the business developer is one of the few individuals within a firm who, almost with impunity, can stick their nose into many aspects of the business. As such, it applies before, during and after a project.

As a "nudger," the business developer asks questions—about everything. Why has something happened? Why has it not? How and when are commitments going to be met? And, if necessary, why have those commitments not been met? What will be required to enable an individual or a project team to fulfill a task or an assignment? It is, of course, essential that the nudger be beyond reproach and that they carry out the responsibilities of their position to satisfy the objectives and expectations of the firm's principals.

As nudger during a project, the business developer's role is always to remind project team members of their critical role in BD as they work through the project with the client. The business developer must continually ask the project team members to provide information. What have they learned about the client, the organization, the business and its future plans? Is there potential work coming up for another group/discipline/office? Has the team informed the client of your other capabilities? What are next steps to ensure that the firm is considered for or selected for the next project?

Some may perceive these questions as threatening. Therefore, as with the coaching role, the business developer's role as nudger demands well-developed interpersonal skills so as not to alienate others within the firm, which would diminish the business developer's effectiveness not only in the role of nudger, but in all other roles as well.

8.3.2 Technical Staff

The pre-eminent internal market in a professional service firm is composed of the technical project staff, those who actually perform the work and charge as much as 100 percent of their time to a client's project. Since the majority of work is (or should be) derived from past or existing clients—estimated at roughly 70 to 90 percent—a firm's fortunes rise or fall on the quality of its technical staff.

Technical staff members play an essential marketing function that is the key underpinning of a successful firm. Once a client has been contracted and the project work begins, technical staff members have the most direct, frequent, and continuous exposure to clients. Of all staff, technical staff members carry the biggest responsibility for furthering the firm's business.

Good work must be delivered. Clients must be satisfied and expectations met. As intermediaries between client and firm, the technical staff members must deliver outstanding service that will maintain business and engender future project opportunities with clients confident about the firm's work.

As a benefit and enhancement for its technical staff, George Butler Associates established an innovative training program called "Marketing University." The idea,

first conceived during an annual retreat of the firm's marketing department, was a high-quality, multi-dimensional program consisting of specific programs on such topics as networking, cold calling, presentations, ethics and trade shows, among others.

Westlake Reed Leskosky Architects holds weekly project director and managers meetings at which key projects are reviewed and discussed. This has proven to be a good way to keep everyone "in the loop" and educate all levels of staff about the firm's efforts on many fronts.

In truth, the technical staff functions as "client account managers," responsible for maintaining and advancing valuable client relationships. It could be argued that this is their most important role in the firm. Since the firm is now part of a client's life cycle, it is up to the technical staff member to maintain the life cycle and minimize (if not eliminate) future competition.

Client account managers, says veteran public relations consultant Joan Capelin, FSMPS, Hon. AIA, of Capelin Communications, "understand what will make a client happy but, even more significantly, what a client's worst fears are."

Capelin encourages internal marketing that is expressly tailored to the technical staff on a project team. Writing in DesignIntelligence and in her book, Communication by Design, she recommends that specific information be shared with project staff, such as:

- The project's mission, so far as the client is concerned
- The reason the job was sought
- The reason the assignment came to the firm
- What was promised to the clients, and why
- What definition of success pertains
- Whether a public project has special requirements

More generally, internal marketing focuses on the technical staff by providing special training, information and motivation in specific areas that need improvement. Those areas may include:

- Presentations
- Verbal communications
- Nonverbal communications such as posture, gestures, personal image and dress
- Technical or proposal writing
- Negotiations or conflict resolution
- Project initiation and maintenance
- Client contact
- Leadership development
- Time management
- Team building

8.3.3 Senior Management

Another important internal market comprises the firm's executives and senior managers—the group ultimately responsible for hiring and firing, and building and maintaining business. Whether they make the initial call, close a deal at the culmination of the client capture effort, negotiate the contract, or go on to participate in the execution of the project, they are crucial targets of internal marketing.

Senior management sets the tone. They lead by doing. They set strategy and lead in the implementation phase, hopefully in an atmosphere of mutual trust and respect. They empower others to realize their dreams and ambitions. Personifying the firm's values and credibility, executive and senior managers foster a corporate culture that is strong and creative enough for internal marketing to take root and thrive. They nurture an environment in which everyone wants to contribute to its success.

The one essential condition to any successful internal marketing initiative, however, is this: without a top firm executive who demonstrates that it is a priority, internal marketing is doomed to failure. Without a doubt, it is imperative to obtain—and sustain—the support of top management.

"Firm leadership must set the example," says Walter P Moore's Ray Messer. "Leaders should engage staff in ongoing relationship building. When staff sees the 'big guy' doing it with zeal, they will get infected with enthusiasm to maintain relationships and win the next job."

W. Bruce Lea III of Gilbane Building Company and a former SMPS national president agrees. "If the top executive is not involved, if they do not demonstrate that participation in marketing and BD is a prerequisite for both advancement in the firm and better compensation, and if they don't make sales and marketing the first agenda item on any meeting of principals, no matter what you do, you will get a short-term result that will eventually stall and fail—much like pushing a rope?"

"It's the CEO's job to provide the motivation—through behavior and policy, as well as words—for the long term." James J. Moynihan, AIA, CEO of Heery International, practices what he preaches. He actively participates in "Heery University," an ongoing training program, involving both local and regional staff from the firm's 29 offices as well as other executives. By so doing, he proves that with the right leadership, with executive buy-in and support, internal marketing will flourish and take root deep in the culture of a firm and that, conversely, without the right leadership, internal marketing will fail.

Internal marketing focuses on executives and senior managers by engaging them to ensure that current work yields future work, and that the full resources of the firm are positioned to work effectively on behalf of its external markets. Those areas typically include:

- Closing strategies
- Leadership development
- Negotiating or conflict resolution

- Contracts and legal administration
- Effective communications
- Consensus-building
- Motivation
- Time and risk management

8.3.4   Nontechnical Support Staff

A third key internal market in professional service firms is the nontechnical support staff—those who support the firm's work (the administrative, financial, information technology, training and HR groups) and typically do not charge their time to a client's project. They play a critical, necessary function that varies in impact from role to role, as shown in the following examples.

- The receptionist (the so-called "director of first impressions") often has the first crucial contact with clients, prospects, and visitors
- The project assistant facilitates communication between the project team and clients
- The project accountant manages billings between project managers and clients
- The HR representative works for the team's overall well-being
- The office manager keeps everything running smoothly

Nontechnical support staff members contribute to a firm's future by doing just what their title suggests: providing organizational and other support to the executives and technical professionals with whom they work and ensuring a smooth operation. Nontechnical support staff also can contribute to a firm's success through direct and indirect exposure to clients, vendors, referral sources, prospects and visitors to the firm.

Internal marketing focuses on nontechnical staff by providing special training, information, and motivation in specific areas that need improvement. Those areas may include:

- Performance and productivity
- Computer operations
- Database development and management
- Telephone etiquette
- Interpersonal communications
- Working as a team
- Health and safety
- Vendor/supplier relationships
- Benefits management
- Personal image and attire

8.4   Assess and Develop BD Talent

Although every member of a firm has an important role to play in BD, some people will undoubtedly be more talented than others. Identify individuals who have the potential to become a rainmaker in your firm—those people who don't get stuck in the Valley of Death, and seem to have a knack for the rainmaking system described earlier in this section.

Once you've figured out who in your firm (and it may be multiple people) has the most potential to become a powerful BD force, schedule a meeting with them to sit down and create a Professionall Development Plan toward that end. In fact, do this for every staff member who you've identified as people who should be involved in BD activities. Work together to set goals, and develop a plan for how and when those goals will be accomplished. Help them create spreadsheets (or some other tool) that they can use to track their progress.

TARGET POINT

The importance of frequent communication cannot be overstressed! Meet/email/talk with each person regularly to ensure that progress is being made, and to provide encouragement and make any adjustments to their Personal Development Plan.

Review the results of their efforts together and use those results to set goals for the next period. Make sure that you communicate these results with your senior management so that your staff can be rewarded for good work. Depending on how your firm is structured, the marketing director may not have the ability to compensate or reward staff directly, so communicating with upper management (even as high up as firm principals) is important for making sure your staff is recognized.

Give your staff plenty of opportunities to practice and improve their BD skills through presentation, marketing and sales training. Toastmasters—a nonprofit organization with clubs that meet locally to practice skills that will improve their members' public speaking, communication and leadership abilities—is one good training resource. Some firms require their employees to compete in Toastmasters, while others start an informal "in-house" Toastmasters group to make sure that everyone gets frequent practice standing up and speaking in front of a group.

Help employees build their personal brand to market their talents, skills and abilities. Developing a personal brand is essential to standing out in today's marketplace—it tells the world who you are, what you do and how you are different. Your employees need to develop personal brands tied to their unique skill set or experiences—they need to position themselves as experts and thought leaders. As an A/E/C marketer, you need to identify the key staff at your company and work with them, one-on-one, to enhance their reputations. They won't do it on their own, but if you lead them down the path, some (but not all) will follow. Those who do follow will become a critical asset to your company's marketing program, and they should be integrated into your marketing effort.

Many tools can be used to brand a person. Myriad tools are available to build and then maintain a reputation:

- Active involvement in community, professional and client organizations can significantly impact a person's brand

- Writing articles and speaking at meetings, events and conferences brand people as leaders in their fields

- Public relations is not just a tool for corporate branding, but also an effective one for personal branding

- Mentoring, networking and gaining references and endorsements are highly effective tools

Used properly, social media can also be an effective tool to promote your firm's star professionals and the thought leadership they offer clients. LinkedIn is one of the first places a potential client is likely to go to learn more about a member of your staff and their profile must therefore sell their personal brand. Information about their experience and education should be complete and up-to-date; their picture should be appropriate and portrait-style; and their summary should be professional but engaging, revealing something about their professional style and character. To make sure that your employee's profile is high on the list of search results, think of the search terms your ideal client would use and be sure those terms are found throughout the profile.

As part of your marketing program, sit down with your key staff and perform a reputational gap analysis. Ask questions that will identify where these individuals can use some help enhancing their reputations. Then, help them utilize the tools mentioned above to develop a personal marketing plan that will enhance their reputation, advance their career and expand their network—and differentiate your company.

8.5   Key Terms

Below are the main terms covered in this section:

- Business development (BD)
- Rainmaker
- Valley of Death
- Sales Success Cycle
- Rainmaking system
- Curve of Relationships©
- Internal marketing

9   Case Study Activity

This Case Study Activity allows you to reflect on and apply the key concepts that you learned in this Domain to a real-world scenario. Each Domain includes a scenario about the same organization, Gilmore & Associates. The scenario is presented to you, followed by several questions. You can also elect to view the recommended solutions/ responses for each question posed, which are located on the next page.

This case study can be used in many ways:

- You can individually reflect on the questions after reading the scenario, and write your own notes/responses to each question. You can then check your ability to apply the key concepts against the recommended solutions/responses.

- You can pull together a small group and use this scenario to drive a discussion around the challenge and to discuss solutions as a group.

- You can combine a selection of the case study activities (across the Domains) into a larger scenario-based activity as a part of a professional development event.

Thanks in large part to your efforts as the marketing coordinator, Gilmore & Associates has successfully transitioned into a new market. The firm used to only be known for designing K–12 educational facilities, but with a few high-visibility retirement community projects under its belt, it's begun to establish itself as an expert in this niche of older adult healthcare.

Firm leadership has recognized your role in this transition by offering you a management position. You agree to take on the responsibility of coordinating the efforts of staff and consultants to accomplish marketing goals and objectives, and ensure that every step in the sales process—from BD to writing a proposal—continues to run smoothly.

1.   What are some processes that you could put into place to ensure the best possible outcomes for your marketing staff's performance?

2.   What should be included in a pipeline report to help you track activity, hold your team accountable and ultimately help your firm reach its annual growth goals?

3.   You notice that many members of your team express discomfort with their BD role. How can you create a training program that will build the skills that they need to develop more confidence in this role?

4.   One of your team members has decided to go back to school to study nursing and you need to hire someone to fill the open marketing associate position. What can you do to make your firm an appealing choice to job seekers?

5.   What steps can you take to promote a firm-wide BD culture?

Answer Key

1. What are some processes that you could put into place to ensure the best possible outcomes for your marketing staff's performance?

   o Set clear expectations. Measure each staff member's knowledge areas and skill sets, and, based on those results, develop metrics by which they will be evaluated. Also encourage them to gain additional training and certifications, where needed.

   o Provide opportunities for your staff to find a mentor or coach. These relationships can greatly enhance their professional development over both the long and short term.

   o Establish clear lines of communication and provide regular feedback. Have regular team meetings about current and planned activities, as well as more informal one-on-one discussions about how each person is performing.

   o Help them to develop a PDP that identifies a path for their individual professional development within the organization.

2. What should be included in a pipeline report to help you track activity, hold your team accountable, and ultimately help your firm reach its annual growth goals?

   o Information about each lead, including which staff member brought it to your firm's attention, which staff member will head follow-up activities and whether the lead is a previous client or a prospective one

   o Information about the market and service sector that potential new work is associated with

   o A rough approximation of how much revenue that the project might bring into your firm and how much it will cost to pursue it

   o How likely you are to win the work based on what you know about the opportunity

3. You notice that many members of your team express discomfort with their BD role. How can you create a training program that will build the skills that they need to develop more confidence in this role?

   o Recognize that some people will never be completely comfortable demonstrating a particular skill—for example, speaking in public or writing proposals. Encourage your staff to focus on enhancing skills within their natural abilities and comfort zone. However, be sure to differentiate between people who will always hate networking (or some other skill) and those who just need more training to succeed.

o   Conduct a training needs assessment via observation, individual interviews and group questionnaires to determine in what areas your team is strong and where they could use additional instruction.

o   Develop a regular schedule of training opportunities. Include both formal and informal (e.g., lunch and learns) training opportunities at appropriate frequencies.

o   Make sure that the training sessions are hands-on and simulate the real world. For a training session on proposal writing, have participants write a sample proposal. For one on interviews, conduct a mock interview.

o   Create a maintenance plan so that the training schedule is not dropped once your employees attend the initial sessions. For long-lasting improvement, people must have regular opportunities to practice learned skills.

4. One of your team members has decided to go back to school to study nursing, and you need to hire someone to fill the open marketing associate position. What can you do to make your firm an appealing choice to job seekers?

o   Offer to help HR develop attractive and well-written job announcements for various mediums.

o   Know what motivates the people who will be searching for a job in your industry—this includes an interest in the work, opportunity for growth, a sense of accomplishment and earned recognition—and tailor your recruitment announcements to address these needs.

o   Consider the target audience for the job opening. A marketing associate is an entry-level position, so your candidates are more likely to be recent graduates in the Millennial Generation than Baby Boomers.

o   Make sure that your web site is up-to-date and attractive, and that the "Apply for a Job" tab is easy to find from the home page.

o   Consider setting up a booth at college career fairs. Sell the culture of your firm at the booth and select staff that will relate well to Millennials.

5. What steps can you take to promote a firm-wide BD culture?

o   Recognize that it takes time for BD efforts to show obvious pay-offs and encourage your staff to view the development of client relationships as a long-term and continuous effort, as opposed to a task that is only done when the firm needs new business.

o   Include sales training in your firm training program so that your team develops good selling habits.

o   Set standards that give staff the discipline needed to push through the initial period of discouragement. For example, ask them to make 10 calls per week to potential leads, or to collect five new business cards per month.

o   Stress that the goal of BD activities is to develop a relationship, rather than making a sale. Project opportunities will follow the formation of a good relationship.

o   Make sure that the roles and responsibilities of each staff member are clearly defined.

o   Get buy-in from senior management so that successful BD efforts are recognized from the top and given an appropriate reward.

10   Glossary

Accounts Receivable Collections
The average number of days it takes to collect from clients for service.

Amount (Column)
A three-part column in the pipeline report that represents an estimate of the fee associated with a potential project. This number is a rough approximation based on initial thoughts or conversations about what the prospect/client might need, and is recorded in either the "idea," "made contact," or "proposal" column depending on what stage the sale is in.

Arbitration
The use of a third party to settle a dispute.

Baby Boomers
The generation composed of people born between the mid-1940s and early 1960s.

Backlog
The work (revenue) logged which has yet to be completed.

Business Development (BD)
1.   The gathering and compilation of client and pursuit knowledge in advance of a request for proposals through direct interaction with the client.
2.   Activities that you or your firm performs to win projects with a customer or prospect including calls, visits, correspondence, electronic communications, entertainment, referrals, trade shows and the like.

Business Unit/Niche (Column)
A column in the pipeline report that documents what industry niche or business unit potential new work will be associated with.

Charge-Out Rate
Staff hourly rate + (Staff hourly rate x Company overhead rate) + Profit

Chief Information Officer (CIO)
Senior member of the firm who serves as the bridge between the information systems department and the company's top management.

Client/Prospect (Column)
A column in the pipeline report that documents whether a sale was to a repeat client (client) or prospective client (prospect).

Coach
The person who takes on a teaching role to improve the student's performance in a concrete issue or skill set.

Consequential Damages
Damages that are not directly caused by one party's breach of a contract, but which may result from the breach. Legal principles allow for parties to a contract to agree to waive their right to collect these types of damages in the event of a breach.

Consideration
The value exchanged between the two parties in a contract. It can consist of promises, services, goods and/or money.

Contract
1.   A mutually binding legal relationship obligating the seller to furnish the supplies or services (including construction) and the buyer to pay for them. It includes all types of commitments that obligate the government to an expenditure of appropriated funds and that, except as otherwise authorized, are in writing (Source: FAR Part 2.101).
2.   An exchange of promises, either orally or in writing, between two or more parties that creates a legal obligation between them.

Cross-Functional Training
Training conducted in such a way that the staff of each functional area is well-versed on the needs and opportunities presented by their teammates in the other department.

Cross-Selling
Selling a different service offered by your firm to an existing client.

Current Ratio
The ratio of the firm's current assets (for example, cash, accounts receivable, unbilled services, notes receivable, prepaid expenses) to its current liabilities.

Curve of Relationships©
A model developed by Blackridge, Ltd. that describes the relationship-building process by defining five levels of connection and three phases of evolution.

Customer Relationship Management (CRM)
A multi-faceted process, mediated by a set of information technologies (such as databases) that focuses on creating two-way exchanges with customers so that firms have an intimate knowledge of their needs, wants and buying patterns. In this way, CRM is intended to help companies understand, as well as anticipate, the needs of current and potential customers.

Decision Support System (DSS)
A DSS consists of software that enables managers to access the information in a company's database dynamically, to produce customized reports on an as-needed basis to assist in decision making. It combines the company's data systems and commercial databases, specialized modeling software, and a graphical user interface (typically in the form of a dashboard for usability and system interactivity).

Doer-Closer
A senior-level member of the firm who focuses on marketing existing clients and spends most of their time on billable projects.

Financial Statement
A document that provides an overview of how money is moving through a company. Generally includes a balance sheet and a profit/loss or revenue/expense statement.

Firm Offer
An offer that is limited as to the length of time it will remain open for acceptance.

Gen X

The generation composed of people born between the mid-1960s and early 1980s.

Human Resources (HR)
The department responsible for the framework of employment—policies, procedures, guidelines, compensation and benefits—as well as talent development and training.

Idea (Column)
A column in the pipeline report that the fee estimate goes into if your firm has not had any conversations with the targeted client yet, but thinks there is a potential opportunity.

Inbound Marketing
The practice of participating in a dialogue with clients through social media, content sharing and other tools.

Information Sharing
The practice of sharing valuable information with people in your network.

Internal Marketing
A multi-dimensional strategy for growing a firm from the inside out, focusing sharply on the people inside a firm. It is a continuous, participative process that fosters training and motivation of employees—principally those with client contact.

Knowledge Management
The process by which organization knowledge is captured, stored and disseminated within a company.

Lead
An indication or a clue to a potential project.

Lead Originator
The person who brought a new opportunity/lead to the firm.

Lead Tracking System
A system that documents potential new opportunities and clients.

Lunch and Learn
Short training sessions that occur during regular business hours, where lunch is provided for the staff.

Made Contact (Column)
A column in the pipeline report that the fee estimate goes into if your firm has started conversations with the targeted client and plans to follow up.

Management Information System (MIS)
A system that uses information from the company's database to produce standardized reports on a regular basis.

Mediation
A procedure in which the parties submit their dispute, including the details of their position, to an independent third-party mediator.

Mentor
The individual that takes on the teaching role in the long-term development of a professional relationship between two people that fosters trust, confidence and mutual learning.

Millennials
The generation composed of people born between the mid-1980s and early 2000s.

Net Multiplier
The ratio of net revenues (generated by in-house labor only, without reimbursable expenses) to total direct labor (raw labor salary only, without any fringe benefits).

Net Profit Ratio
The ratio of net profit (income minus expenses) to net revenues.

Networking
Gaining and giving information with those which might assist you in doing a better job, in your work or in your life.

Overhead Rate
The ratio of overhead costs (operating expenses not assigned to projects, including indirect salaries) to total direct labor.

Personal Development Plan (PDP)
A document that outlines an employee's plans for personal development over the next year.

Pipeline Amount
A number in the pipeline report that is calculated by multiplying the value of the engagement by the probability of close.

Pipeline Report
A report that measures current pending sales opportunities weighted by the probability of closing the sale.

Probability of Close
A rough estimate of the likelihood (expressed as a percentage) that a lead will eventually become closed new business.

Proposal (Column)
A column in the pipeline report that the fee estimate goes into if the targeted client is interested in talking with your firm and has asked for a fee estimate or a formal proposal.

Rainmaker
A professional, usually a partner, who both generates leads and converts them into work for his firm at levels outstripping the others partners to such a degree that it appears miraculous.

Rainmaking system
A four-point intervention process developed to give professionals the skills, standards, systems and support needed to become a rainmaker.

Sales Success Cycle
A model that describes the stage of client development where small successes, self-motivation and self-confidence feed off each other to become a self-sustaining cycle of success.

Scope of Work
The nature of the project. Also, the document that describes the project in terms recognizable by both the client and the A/E/C professional.

Seller-Doer
Technical professional, generally a firm principal, responsible for making the sale and doing the work.

Service (Column)
A column in the pipeline report that is used to determine who can help with sales efforts and to track whether a firm is working a balance of opportunities.

SMART Goals
An acronym that defines the characteristics of achievable goals, SMART stands for specific, measurable, attainable, relevant and time-bound.

Sponsorship
Giving financial support to an organization or group.

Staff Utilization Ratio
The ratio of a firm's total direct labor to its total labor (all salaries, including fringe benefits).

Strengths, Weaknesses, Opportunities, and Threats (SWOT) Analysis
A situational analysis tool that is based on assessing the strengths, weaknesses, opportunities and threats that your firm faces, either as a whole or in a specific market.

Target Multiplier
The ratio of an employer's charge-out rate to his or her payroll rate.

User Group
The people who will be using a software system.

Valley of Death
The typically discouraging early stage of client development during which the amount of time and effort a person puts into development activities does not seem to be reflected in their results.

Working Lead

The person who will direct the follow-up activity for an opportunity/lead. May or may not be the same person as the lead originator.

11   Related Resources

Knowledge Assessment Tool:

"Blueprints: Guides for Marketing and Business Development Departments in the A/E/C Industry," published by SMPS

Mentoring and Coaching:

The Language of Leadership: Stories and Studies in Courage, Wisdom, and Sacrifice, by Louis L. Marines, 2010

Rainmaking:

Creating Rainmakers: The Manager's Guide to Training Professionals to Attract New Clients, by Ford Harding, 2006

Rain Making: Attract New Clients No Matter What Your Field, by Ford Harding, 2008

12 Figures

13 Index

14   About the Photographer:

Andrew Buchanan is an architectural, interior, aerial, and land design photographer in Seattle, WA, Photographing the Spaces Where We Live, Work, and Play®. Buchanan offers compelling, graphic photography of built environments to design and marketing professionals, hotels and resorts, developers, magazines, and advertisers across the West Coast. Since 1996, he's believed that working with a photographer should be creative, collaborative, and efficient. A member of SMPS Seattle, Buchanan's website is www.subtlelightphoto and he can be reached at andrew@subtlelightphoto.com.

15   Peer Review:

The following professionals have peer reviewed one or more domains of the MARKENDIUM: The SMPS Body of Knowledge.

Ed Hannan, Executive Editor

Janet Brooks, CPSM
Cynthia Jackson, FSMPS, CPSM
Francis Lippert, FSMPS, CPSM
Fawn Radmanich, CPSM
Julie Shepard, CPSM, ENV SP
Andrea Story, CPSM

16 Body of Knowledge Subject Matter Experts (SMEs)

Dana L. Birkes, APR, FSMPS, CPSM

CMO, Clifford Power Systems, Tulsa, OK

Scott W. Braley, FAIA, FRSA

Principal Consultant, Braley Consulting & Training, Atlanta, GA

Theresa M. Casey, FSMPS, CPSM

Principal, On Target Marketing & Communications LLC, Columbia, CT

Karen O. Courtney, AIA, FSMPS

Chief Marketing Officer, Fanning Howey, Indianapolis, IN

Dana Galvin Lancour, FSMPS, CPSM

Director of Communications, Barton Malow Company, Southfield, MI

Shannah A. Hayley, FSMPS, CPSM

Director of Marketing and Community Engagement, City of Plano, Plano, TX

Linda M. Koch, FSMPS, CPSM

Director of Marketing & Business Development, Pfluger Architects, San Antonio, TX

Michael J. Reilly, FSMPS

Principal, Reilly Communications, Boston, MA

Laurie B. Strickland, FSMPS, CPSM

Director of Marketing, Nitsch Engineering, Boston, MA

Mark Tawara, FSMPS, CPSM

Owner, Manageability, LLC, Kailua, HI

Nancy J. Usrey, FSMPS, CPSM

Associate Vice President, HNTB Design Build, Plano, TX

Andrew J. Weinberg, FSMPS, CPSM

Regional Business Development Manager, Simpson Gumpertz & Heger Inc., New York, NY